## *Predeparture prepping on how to live and make money in a new culture*

**Emerging** (*i merj ing*) or **Developing** (*di vel o ping*) **Countries** - *Countries where one can go to benefit from the low cost of living and tremendous business opportunities.*

The Official Guide Book Series reports on countries where couples can live on around $1,000 per month and start a business on a shoestring.

The OG Book Series is devoted to adventurous expatriates who choose to pursue their dreams in emerging markets, seeking business opportunities, retirement or just a change of lifestyle.

Don't miss these other Living and Making Money Books brought to you exclusively by OG Books Worldwide:

Mexico
Caribbean
Central America
Cuba

Created and directed by Robert Lawrence Johnston III

# OFFICIAL GUIDE
# LIVING & MAKING MONEY
# IN
# Costa Rica

**Official Guide Books
Worldwide**

Published By:
Official Guide Books
Worldwide
PO Box 2062
Vashon Island, Washington 98070
WWW.livingoverseas.com
Tel: 800-341-2510, ext. 27

Copyright ©1997 by Official Guide Books Worldwide. Previous editions copyright © 1993, 1994, 1995, 1996. All rights reserved. This book or parts thereof may not be reproduced in any form without permission.

Printed in the United States of America

Costa Rica

ISBN: 9968-9779-3-4

## ABOUT THE OFFICIAL GUIDE BOOK SERIES

The Official Guide Book Series is published by Official Guide Books Worldwide, a leading publisher of overseas living and business start-up guides for the enterprising individual and small business owner. Our books feature countries where couples can live on around $1,000 per month and economically start a small business that can grow into a global enterprise.

Today's global economy is opening the doors to opportunity that only a decade ago would have seemed an unattainable dream. Improvements in technology and telecommunications make it easier than ever to live in Costa Rica and operate a secretarial and translation service, or in Mexico, running an English-language bookstore, or on a Caribbean island, operating a mail order business. Today's global marketplace knows no geographical borders.

Our guide books will explain why now is the best time to venture abroad and prosper. We will help you get established in anticipation of the new millennium and the tremendous opportunities that will follow.

The staff at OG Books Worldwide is committed to publishing quality, fun books that meet your needs. Our writers are all longtime expatriates who have personally experienced life abroad and have discovered the secrets to forging a successful business there.

Whether this is your first experience with OG books or you're a regular reader, we want to hear from you! Tell us what you think of this edition and give us suggestions. Let us know what we should do to make the book more useful for you. Drop us a line through e-mail and be sure to visit our **World Wide Web site at WWW.livingoverseas.com** for updated profiles on overseas money-making opportunities.

# ACKNOWLEDGMENTS AND DEDICATION

We owe thanks to all those who helped with the research and preparation of our fifth edition.

Special thanks to Audrey McDermott, Rosemary McDermott and Melissa Liscano at TEMPO S.A. for their translation and secretarial expertise their company provided.

For sharing their expertise and the time they took from their very busy schedules to help write this book we thank:

        Gerardo Chávez    Mike Garrett
        David Garrett     Fiona Martin
        Peter Bernnan    Ellen Ruticoff

Extra special thanks go to Amy González for her friendly assistance with sales, marketing and collections, and to Christine Pratt for the hours she spent, editing, rewriting, updating, and giving the book a professional and friendly touch. To Morgan Hicks thank you for the "eye of scrutiny" given to the final, and last minute production details.

This book, the first in our series, is dedicated to the two people who without their love and support this book and company could never have gotten off the ground, my Mother, Patricia Ann Kilpatrick, and my Grandma, "Grumps" Doris Rodriquez. Also, to my two wonderful sisters, Karyn Snell and Cheryl Broderick whose help these past few years was invaluable, and to my adventurous girlfriend, Teresa Galvan for "Living and Making Money in Mexico and Central America" with me.

# ABOUT THIS BOOK

The *Official Guide to Living and Making Money in Costa Rica* will tell you what you need to know about succeeding in business and in life in one of the most popular travel and living destinations in the world today.

You don't need to be a worldly traveler with a big bank account to succeed in this tiny, peaceful Central American country. Thanks to OG Books, an analysis of the living and business environment is no longer like working a jigsaw puzzle with a couple of pieces missing -- we provide you with the missing pieces!

This book will tell you:

- ✓ Why now is the best time to set your sights abroad
- ✓ Secret tips from longtime expat's
- ✓ How to prosper in Costa Rica either full or part-time
- ✓ How to start a business for less than $3,000
- ✓ How you can live for around $1,200 per month
- ✓ How to move your furniture and ship your car
- ✓ Where to send your kids to school
- ✓ Where to live

**AND MORE!**

All you need is an adventurous spirit, a little guts and this book to live a challenging but exciting international lifestyle in the tropics.

# CONTENTS

**ABOUT THE OFFICIAL GUIDE BOOK SERIES**............................... v

**ACKNOWLEDGMENTS**........................................................... vi

**ABOUT THIS BOOK**................................................................ vii

**FOREWORD**.......................................................................... 10

**COSTA RICA PROFILE**........................................................... 12
Map of Costa Rica

**OVERSEAS ENTREPRENEUR**..................................................... 14

**ABOUT COSTA RICA**............................................................. 19
Country · History · Government · Economy · People · Climate

**GLOBAL LIVING AND INVESTING INDEX**................................... 28

**10 QUICK TIPS FOR THE NEWCOMER**..................................... 31

**GENERAL INFORMATION**....................................................... 34
Cost of Living · Salaries · Working · Business Hours · Bureaucracy · Corruption · Pay Offs · Post Office · Telephones · Bills · Currency · Language · Banking · Tourist Entry and Exit · Holidays · Newspapers · Health · Utilities · Clothing · Transportation · Numbering of Streets · Greetings · Gifts · Social Events · Tipping · Domestic Employees · Bringing your Pets · Casinos · Crime · Social Life · Restaurants · Shopping · Supermarkets · Matrimony · Adoption · Surnames · Theaters · Television/Cable · Theaters · Clubs · Better Business Bureau · Religion · Duty Free Zone · Driving · Radio Stations

**LIFE AS AN EXPATRIATE**....................................................... 61

**REAL ESTATE**....................................................................... 66
Places to Live · Speculating · How to Buy · Beaches · Laws · Squatters · Building a Home · Registration · Brokers · Closing Costs · Devaluation · Rentals

**HEALTH OPTIONS**................................................................ 90
Diseases · Hospitals and Doctors · Plastic Surgery · Dental Care

**MEDICAL INSURANCE**.......................................................... 102
Policy Costs · Cost Deductibles · How to Buy Insurance · Int'l Coverage

**MAKING MONEY.................................................................. 115**
   Why Invest · Obtaining Investment Information · Who are the Consumers? · Overseas Entrepreneur · Small Business Options · Starting Tips · For the Passive Investor

**SMALL BUSINESS START UPS.......................................... 133**
   How to Own a Business · Business Ideas · Franchises · On-Line Systems · A Word of Caution · Buying an Existing Business · Labor Law

**THE PEOPLE WHO'VE DONE IT............................................. 155**

**BANKING.............................................................................. 166**
   Public and Private Banks · Checking and Savings Accounts

**TAXES.................................................................................. 172**
   Income Tax · Tax Haven · U.S. Tax Laws · Capital Gains · Sales & Vehicle Tax

**OFFSHORE CORPORATIONS............................................. 178**
   What is an Offshore Corporation · How & Why Establish One · Privacy

**FINDING A GOOD LAWYER................................................. 182**
   Why you Need a Lawyer · Where to Find a Good Lawyer

**RESIDENCY......................................................................... 185**
   Retired · Earning Residents · Investor · Company · Visas · Work Permits

**SCHOOLS............................................................................. 196**
   Primary and Secondary · Universities · Spanish Schools

**MOVING FURNITURE........................................................... 204**

**BRINGING YOUR CAR.......................................................... 207**

**AUTO INSURANCE............................................................... 211**

**OBTAINING A DRIVER'S LICENSE...................................... 215**

**COSTA RICAN CONSULATES AND EMBASSIES............... 216**

**CLUBS, GROUPS & ORGANIZATIONS............................... 218**

**SUGGESTED READING....................................................... 221**

**EMERGENCY PHONE NUMBERS....................................... 223**

**SOURCES USED IN COMPILING THIS BOOK.................... 224**

**CLASSIFIED ADVERTISERS................................................ 225**

# FOREWORD

When many people visit Costa Rica for the first time, they fall in love with the country's beautiful countryside, the tropical beaches, perfect climate and friendly people.

The idea of living in Costa Rica as a business owner, retiree or as a person seeking a change of lifestyle is alluring for many good reasons. The cost of living is lower than in the United States or Canada. A modern, first-rate medical and dental system rates up near the U.S. and Canada as one of the best in the world. The business climate is stable and can be very profitable, and democracy is one of the most cherished traditions, along with the sense of individual liberty and freedom.

Costa Rica offers enormous growth potential that most North Americans are unaware of. A couple can live comfortably for around $1,200 per month and start a business on a shoestring without prohibitive regulations or taxes.

But Costa Rica has problems like anywhere else. In fact, one of the biggest problems is that life here can run so smoothly that it's easy to forget you're in a developing country until you hit a snag... and then it's frustrating.

The *Official Guide to Living and Making Money in Costa Rica* has been compiled to ease the newcomer's introduction to Costa Rica. We try to provide up-to-date information, but such things as personal income tax rates, the cost of medical insurance and other government controlled programs are adjusted yearly. Use all figures as guidelines only.

Before you decide to live or invest in Costa Rica, we strongly suggest you plan an extended visit to thoroughly investigate the living conditions and all business options that are best for you. Information is the key to a smooth cultural and economic transition to life in a foreign land.

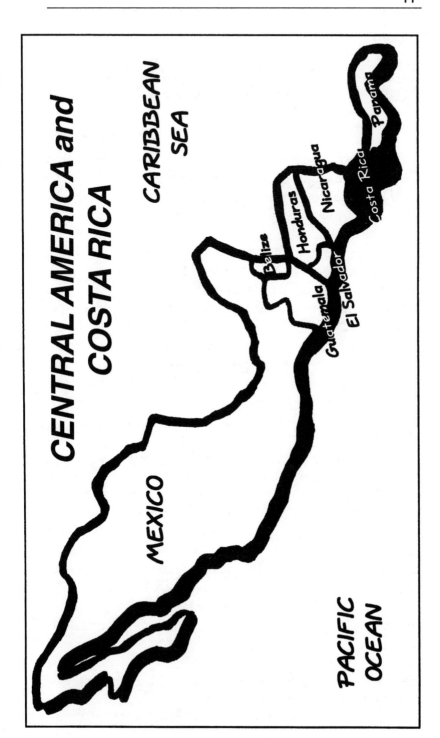

# COSTA RICA PROFILE

| | |
|---|---|
| Official Name: | Republic of Costa Rica |
| Capital City: | San José |
| Population: | 3,350,000 |
| Government: | Republic; based on civil law. |
| Head of State: | José María Figueres (1994-1998). |
| Living environment: | |
| Pro's: | Excellent climate, lower-cost life, friendly people, potable water. |
| Con's: | High import tax, "mañana syndrome," bad roads. |
| Business environment: | |
| Pro's: | Stable government and economy, great opportunities. |
| Con's: | Bureaucracy, and considerable corruption. |
| Local currency: | Colón |
| Exchange rate: | US$1.00=₡217 (January 1997) |
| Inflation: | 13.5% |
| Devaluation: | 15% |
| Unemployment rate: | 4.5% |
| Major traditional export: | Bananas, coffee, meat |
| Leading Generator of Foreign Revenue: | Tourism, textiles, banana, coffee |
| Literacy rate: | 93% |
| Time difference: | Same as central standard time. |
| Foreign population: | More than 20,000. |

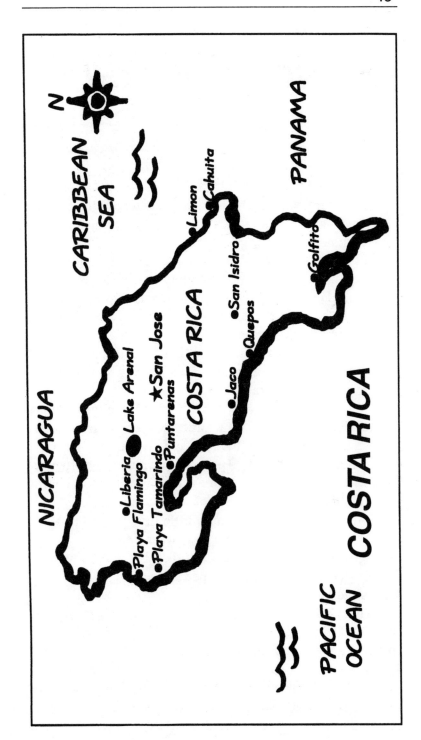

# INTRODUCTION

**Expatriates** *(eks PA tree ats) - Those who leave their costly homeland to live and prosper elsewhere*

I called my friend John the other day to complain of the trials and tribulations of living and working as an expatriate in the tiny country of Costa Rica. John cut me off in mid-sentence and went into a 20 minute tirade about how he and his family were dealing with 10° below zero weather in Detroit. The snow was so deep he couldn't get his car out of the garage to get to his job as manager of a local restaurant.

He said he would rather be selling corn flakes on a street corner and living in a grass hut in the tropics than confronting the proverbial rat race day after day.

He went on to say how lucky I am to live in a country where beer only costs $0.40 a bottle and the weather is nearly always perfect — not to mention how being able to afford live-in help at only $125.00 per month would give him more time with the kids and extra time for long walks on the beach with his wife.

By this time I was getting a little thirsty for that $0.40 bottle of beer. I knew, of course, that he wouldn't be happy selling corn flakes on the street corner, but maybe with his restaurant experience he could open up a small café that serves U.S.-style breakfast and lunches.

After all, even though Costa Rica receives more than 800,000 visitors per year and boasts a foreign population of in excess of 20,000, the country doesn't have a restaurant like that yet. Opportunity really could await him here.

My friend John isn't alone. Many people are disenchanted with their jobs and with the way their lives are heading in general. Effected by company downsizing, low wages, crime and inefficient public schools, many people are fed up and want a career and lifestyle change that they've worked hard to deserve.

And they're doing something about it. They're starting to take control of their lives and pursue their dreams of a quality lifestyle — even if it means braving the new world, leaving the safety net of friends and family behind and setting off to conquer a new language, a new culture and a whole new way of life.

## *OVERSEAS OPPORTUNITIES 2000*

Today, a fax machine, a computer, the internet, a telephone and a little ingenuity are the means to tap the potential wealth of the emerging economies of Latin America and the Caribbean, where emerging markets are yearning for the quality of goods and services taken for granted in developed nations.

Not only that, but the cost of living in countries like Costa Rica is, frankly, cheap. You and your spouse can live well and pay a full or part-time housekeeper for around $1,200 per month. Theaters show first-run movies for around $2.50. A steak dinner with wine costs less than $6.00, and if the meal gives you indigestion, don't worry; a trip to the doctor will only set you back about $25.00. Toothache? A local dentist will take good care of you for around $10.00 per filling.

These exotic tropical countries with their exuberant jungles and pristine beaches offer a host of weekend getaways only hours from home with deluxe accommodations at a fraction of U.S. costs.

**Global Marketplace** *(GLO•bal MAR•ket•plays): a market where production, labor, commerce and resources know no international boundaries.*

In Costa Rica, a hard-working individual can start a business from scratch without facing the cumbersome regulations and high start-up costs encountered back home. The country even offers incentives for investments of national interest, such as reforestation or job-producing export industries.

Foreign entrepreneurs can benefit from their "hindsight of 20/20," as they find that many of the products and services already successful back home would also be successful here — if only the people had access to them. Once they find their niche, they're on their way.

The spot light is on the new millennium, and the individuals who are prepared, will discover opportunities never before imagined.

**Your first step to prospering in our new global marketplace is knowing why *now* is the time to get started. It's simple to understand, once you have the T.O.O.Ls.**

**T**elecommunications - Lap top computers, e-mail, faxes, cellular phones and the internet are leveling the playing field so the "little guy or gal" can compete against the established multinational corporation.

**O**pening of World Markets - National borders are opening up with the removal of restrictive trade barriers, allowing easier access to their markets.

**O**pportunities - Many countries abroad are five to 10 years or more behind the U.S. in many products and services that North Americans take for granted.

**L**ow Cost of Living - Perhaps the greatest advantage of life in a developing country is the low cost of living and low business start-up expenses that allow you to "cultivate" your new endeavor without sacrificing the lifestyle you have grown accustomed to.

The boom in telecommunications, the opening of world markets, the low cost of living and an ample sphere of opportunity provide most of the ingredients that the flexible entrepreneur needs to succeed in Costa Rica.

English has emerged as the common language of international commerce and business. Costa Rica is only two hours flying time to Miami, and the internet makes long-distance correspondence to anywhere in the world faster and cheaper than ever before.

Combine all this with an adventurous spirit and a little guts and it isn't hard to see how the micro-entrepreneur can become an international player — one who has left the 8 to 5 grind back home to meet life head-on, doing something enjoyable, living economically and prospering.

## GLOBAL ENTREPRENEURS

**Bookstore** U.S. citizens John and Mark started an English-language bookstore in San José, the capital of Costa Rica. Using their "tools," they take advantage of the internet to fill many of their orders to avoid high long-distance rates and warehousing charges. The country's low import duties on books allow for competitive prices.

Costa Rica's new-found popularity as an investment, retirement and tourist destination has led to a burgeoning middle-class foreign population.

John and Mark are now planning to publish their own book on the birds and flora of Costa Rica.

**Handicrafts** Harry, a professional business manager, loved his hobby of woodworking so much that after perfecting furniture making techniques, he began studying the art of fine hand tool design and construction.

Today, from his machine and woodworking shop in the west San José suburb of Escazú, he manufactures some of the world's most precise hand tools of top-quality steel, brass and fine Costa Rican hardwoods. He personally trained his team of 16 craftsmen to produce the tools that are then sold in the U.S., Canada, Japan, Europe and South Africa. One of his hand planes was even featured in Penthouse magazine!

**Graphic Design** And then there's Christine, the former Peace Corps volunteer from Oregon who liked Costa Rica so much she stayed and started a successful business in news writing and graphic design. She currently writes for two leading publications, contributes stories to international mediums, designs bilingual brochures and advertising for international firms and even publishes a small language book.

**Construction** Or Rich, the Chicago construction worker who was barely getting by before discovering through a friend that Central America lacked the sophisticated, up-to-date building techniques that U.S. and Canadian builders take for granted.

In just four years and with very little money he was able to build a successful company that imports the latest materials to construct custom homes among the rain forests and tropical beaches of Costa Rica. He's currently eyeing the neighboring markets of Panama and Nicaragua to carry on his success story.

## *WHY WAIT?*

The world is changing fast, and its many opportunities will pass you by unless you act.

Many of us seem to wish for the good old days where life was slower and opportunities seemed to be endless, but those who venture abroad are discovering that the good old days are *now*.

What would you do if you could pioneer a market that was similar to the U.S. 10 to 20 years ago? Would you buy real estate? Start a small business with hopes of international expansions or just enjoy the inexpensive living and ideal climate of a tropical paradise?

Ask yourself these questions, do some research, make a decision and start packing your bags for a new life abroad. It's not too late!

# ABOUT COSTA RICA

## COUNTRY

About the size of the State of West Virginia, Costa Rica is, surprisingly, one of the most biologically diverse, breathtakingly beautiful and warmly welcoming countries in the world.

In just one weekend, a traveler in Costa Rica can enjoy visiting a white-sand Pacific Ocean beach, hiking through the lush lowland rainforests, rafting down a turbulent river, touring volcanic mountain ranges and watching the sunset over the Caribbean Sea. All this, and be back to the city of San José in time to dance to salsa or merengue in a crowded nightclub!

From North to South or East to West, the country stretches only 200 miles. The shortest distance between oceans is 75 miles. Costa Rica occupies an area of 20,000 square miles and has a population of just over 3 million.

Three mountain ranges divide this Central American country, forming five distinct geographical areas: the Tropical lowlands on the Pacific and Caribbean coasts, the North Central Plains, the median-high Central Valley, and the broad, generally low Northwest Peninsula.

The country's mountainous backbone extends from the northern region to the southern border with Panama, breaking only to accommodate the Central Valley.

A chain of active and dormant volcanoes dots this mountain range, giving rise to steaming thermal springs and occasional earth tremors.

Although more than two-thirds of its boundaries are coastline, 70 percent of Costa Rica's population lives in the Central Valley, where altitudes range from 2,624 to 4,920 feet, averaging about 3,280 feet.

Mount Chirripó at 3,820 meters (12,500 feet) is the highest peak in Costa Rica. While sugarcane and other crops are common here, much of the Central Valley is planted in coffee.

The capital, San José, is located in the Central Valley and home to approximately one-third of the country's inhabitants. Some of the other principal cities in the region include Alajuela, Cartago, and Heredia.

Liberia and Puntarenas, situated in the north and south Pacific regions, and Limón, the main Caribbean port, have large populations as well. There are seven provinces in the country. These include: San José, Alajuela, Cartago, Heredia, Guanacaste, Limón and Puntarenas.

## *HISTORY*

During his final voyage to the New World in 1502, Christopher Columbus anchored off of what is now the Caribbean port city of Limón. Spain then colonized the country they called Costa Rica, or "rich coast," after the thick green tropical foliage he spotted from sea. Costa Rica remained a colony of Spain governed from Guatemala City from 1506-1821.

The cash crops of coffee, bananas and cacao, as well as the gradual arrival of non-Spanish Europeans, opened up trade with the outside world. Coffee was introduced in the early 1800s and was especially suited to the country's climate and soil. By the mid-1800s, coffee was Costa Rica's principal export, and the growers were a powerful and wealthy group.

The first railroad from Limón to the Central Valley was financed by English loans and was completed in 1890. Banana cultivation then started, and the United Fruit Company became a multi-million-dollar enterprise. Agri-business boomed during the 1920s and 30s, and the country was able to pursue the goals of improved health, economy, and education.

The revolution of 1948 marked a turning point in Costa Rican history. War broke out when president Rafael Angel

Calderón Fournier, considered father of the country's health and education systems, refused to relinquish the presidency after losing the election.

José "don Pepe" Figueres led the 40-day rebellion. He exiled vanquished president Calderón, drafted a new constitution that abolished the army and reinstated democratic elections. He later fortified the socialist seeds planted by his predecessor. Figueres would go on to become Costa Rica's most loved political figure. He died in 1992.

Costa Rica is now a model democracy for all of Latin America. The country was nominated twice for a Nobel Peace Prize, and in 1987 former President Oscar Arias was awarded this prestigious award for his key role in organizing a regional peace plan.

## *GOVERNMENT*

Costa Rica's democratic government is divided into four branches: The Executive Branch, which consists of the President, two vice-presidents, and the Presidential Cabinet; the Legislative Branch, composed of the Legislative Assembly with 57 elected representatives; the Judicial Branch, with a Supreme Court and civil and special courts; and the Electoral Tribunal, which is responsible for organizing and supervising elections. Voting rights are acquired at age 18, and women and men have equal rights to elect and be elected.

The President and members of the Legislative Assembly are elected to four-year terms and cannot run for re-election. The two main parties are the United Social Christian Party (PUSC) and the National Liberation Party (PLN). President José María Figueres, son of the fabled "don Pepe," was elected President in 1994. The next elections are slated for 1998, when opposition leader Miguel Angel Rodríguez is expected to be a shoe-in.

The government functions according to two chief sets of guidelines. One set is written in the Constitution and in codes and laws. The other consists of cultural values and norms that also guide decision-making and interaction. Three of the most important provisions of the Constitution are: equality and civil liberties, free elections by secret ballot, and a ban on military forces.

The legal system follows the Civil Law system. It was inspired by the Roman Law and later by the Code Napoleon of France. In recent years it has been influenced by the legislation of Mexico, Argentina, and Spain. Costa Rican law more closely resembles European civil law traditions than the common law traditions of England and the United States.

Foreign policy is based on the concept of non-intervention and the country's unarmed status is guaranteed by international treaties and organizations. Costa Rica is an active member of the United Nations, the International Monetary Fund, and the World Bank.

## *ECONOMY*

Since 1993, tourism has been Costa Rica's leading earner of foreign currency followed closely by textiles, bananas and coffee.

However tourism, which has been described as the country's "economic motor," is showing worrisome trends. Through September 1996, the industry was experiencing growth of -3.2 -- way down from the early 1990s boom years when tourism grew at an astounding 20 percent per year. Figures for October were unofficial at press time, but slightly better.

**Inflation** through October of 1996 reached 11.54 percent and was expected to be 13.5 percent by year's end.

The devaluation rate for 1996 was expected to be 15 percent, with the colón at 218 per $1.00 U.S. by the beginning of 1997. The government will continue its mini-devaluation of 12 céntimos daily at least until the end of 1997.

The policy of mini-devaluations has favored the country's export sector, which demonstrated healthy growth in 1996.

The domestic market is stagnant, however, as Ticos struggle to make their declining salaries stretch to meet their basic needs. Economists are predicting a "zero" gross domestic product (GDP) growth rate for 1996 and most of 1997.

The government has been undergoing a process of liberalization of the economy to enhance the role of the private sector. This is evidenced by the breaking of the banking monopoly, the privatization of the cement company, Cementos del Pacífico S.A. and talk of breaking the insurance monopoly, privatizing the National Liquor Factory and other government-controlled businesses.

The administration of current President José María Figueres raised the sales tax from 10 percent to 15 percent, which applies to all but the most basic of foods and products, and created a 1 percent tax on all corporate assets worth more than ¢30 million ($140,000). Tax collection was greatly improved with the passage of the new Tax Justice Law.

The law authorizes the government to shut down delinquent businesses and throw tax dodgers in prison. Fines will range from ¢48,000 ($223), for not allowing tax inspectors access to books, to ¢4 million ($18,600) for large-scale tax evasion. Violators could also face a prison term of up to 10 years.

**Seeking** help from the international investment community, Costa Rica has promoted foreign investment as part of its development strategy. With the drastic changes in policies, attitudes and structure, the country has gradually improved its standing in the international community.

Government prayers were answered in November 1996, when the high-tech giant Intel announced it would build a 400,000 sq. ft. plant in La Ribera de Belén to test and assemble its Pentium and Pentium Pro line of microprocessors for export. When the plant is fully producing in 1998 it will convert Costa Rica into Latin America's highest per capita exporter.

But the top-heavy public sector still employs more than 60,000 people, including teachers, who are paid from the central government budget. An additional 60,000 are employed by public corporations. The public employees are the most secure and most powerful of salaried workers, and have many organized unions.

**Currently**, the internal debt remains a major obstacle to development. The debt continues to climb as the government sells bonds, mostly to its autonomous State institutions, to finance its consistent budget deficit. The internal debt and its interest payments now consume almost one-third of the GDP.

A special commission of some of the country's top economists were assigned to study the problem in July 1996. They proposed a series of solutions in mid-November that include the sale of some State institutions, increasing taxes and swapping some of the internal debt for external debt at lower interest rates.

The government has been handicapped by the scandal at the nation's oldest bank, Banco Anglo Costarricense, which lost $102 million in bad investments in Venezuelan debt bonds and insider loans to certain customers.

The government closed the bank in September 1994, marking the first time a state-owned bank has been shutdown since the banks were nationalized following the 1948 revolution. Scandal rocked other State banks throughout 1996, when it was revealed that they had granted loans to companies and even political parties that didn't qualify. In some cases, the loans were declared uncollectible and represented million-dollar losses for the banks.

The country cannot count on foreign assistance to improve its infrastructure and social services as it has in the past. The aging Agency for International Development (U.S. AID) finally pulled up stakes for good in 1996, and the administration of U.S. President Bill Clinton has largely ignored the entire region. Countries such as Japan, however, have expressed interest in financing some of the country's internal debt in exchange for a financial "foot" in the Central American "door."

## PEOPLE

Costa Ricans call themselves "Ticos." The affectionate nickname comes from their penchant for adding the diminutive "tico" to all manner of words. For example, a kitten in Spanish anywhere else is "gatito;" in Costa Rica it is a "gatico."

About 95 percent of Ticos are from varying mixtures of the "mestizo" blend of Spanish conquerors and colonists with local indigenous tribes and Jamaican immigrants. The national language is Spanish, although many Ticos speak English, particularly in the Atlantic port city of Limón.

**Democracy** is one of the most cherished traditions along with the sense of individual liberty and freedom. There are more school teachers than policemen and there has not been an army since 1948. Costa Ricans are proud of their peaceful tradition that has stood the test of time and regional turbulence.

A strong family structure exists here and much of the leisure time is spent with relatives and friends. On sunny weekend afternoons, San José's urban parks are bustling with people out for a stroll or just visiting one another. The overwhelming majority of the population is Catholic and church bells can be heard ringing throughout small villages and towns for morning mass. Most couples are married in church and this is usually life long. Divorce is technically legal, but frowned upon. The government contributes money to the church, and religious education is part of the public school curriculum. Formal education is highly valued in this society, and the literacy rate is 93 percent.

Costa Ricans are snappy dressers and take great pride in their appearance and many times spend more than they can afford on the latest up-to-date clothes. They are generally pro-U.S., with U.S. fashions, music and food coming in a close second to the country's traditional fare.

All newcomers will agree that the Costa Ricans are fun-loving people who will go out of their way to help foreigners and make them feel comfortable in their new environment. Visiting a local dance hall on a weekend, you will see people young and old dancing salsa and merengue, eating and drinking and living for today!

While welcoming and friendly, Costa Rica is also home to certain cultural traits that many foreigners may find hard to accept.

Punctuality, for example, is relaxed. It is customary for Ticos to arrive from one-half to one hour late or more for social and business appointments. Bureaucracy and bribery are a ways of life and Costa Ricans are famous procrastinators.

The country's national dish is black beans and rice or "gallo pinto." Genuine Costa Rican specialties are generally enjoyed at home, but one can also sample the local food in a "soda," an informal and inexpensive cafe found in small villages or on nearly every block in San José. The plate of the day is called a "casado," which includes a choice of beef, fish or chicken with rice, beans and plantains. Breakfast and dinner are light, with lunch being the main meal.

Health and longevity in Costa Rica has been improving vastly over the years. The average life expectancy in 1927 was approximately 40 years of age. Currently, the life expectancy for a woman is 77 years and for a man, 72 years. This can be attributed to an overall improvement in health conditions and modern medicine. The Social Security system provides excellent medical care and hospitalization and is available for all Costa Rican citizens.

## *CLIMATE*

Located about 10° north of the equator, the climate of Costa Rica is tropical. There are only two seasons, wet and dry. The dry season, or "verano" (summer) is from December through April. The days are warm and sunny, with clear nights. The rainy season, or "invierno" (winter) is from mid-May to November. An average day in the rainy season usually starts out with warm, sunny mornings and by mid-afternoon clouds appear and one can expect a heavy downpour sometimes lasting into the night. This pattern usually occurs on a daily basis.

Temperatures range from the high 70s to the low 90s and vary depending on the area. Major cities located in the highlands such as San José, Cartago, Alajuela, and Heredia average temperatures in the low 70s Fahrenheit (about 22° centigrade) throughout the year.

On the Pacific Coast, the climate is hotter. Puntarenas, for example, has daytime temperatures in the 90s year round. The Atlantic Coast has more precipitation, with the Atlantic port city of Limón averaging 118-177 inches of rain per year. Temperatures are usually as hot on the Pacific, with a higher percentage of humidity. March and April are the warmest months in Costa Rica and November through January are the coolest. The higher altitudes may get frost above 2,150 meters (7,000 feet).

## ¡PURA VIDA!

*If you're going to make the move, it's best to learn a little Spanish first.*

*Tica and Gringo*

# THE OFFICIAL GUIDE SERIES
## Global Living & Investing Index

Rating a country on its livability or opportunities is based on many factors. In some countries, the benefit of a low cost of living is frequently offset by substandard health conditions or consistently inclement weather. Based on extensive interviews with long-time expatriates living in-country, we at OG books have concocted a scoring system designed to give you an idea of overall conditions.

The categories are ranked on a scale of one to 10, with 10 being excellent. You can then compare how close the country's total score comes to the perfect score of 50, a mythical living and investing utopia.

## CATEGORIES

### Cost of Living  (score: 7)

It's soaring real estate prices, 15 percent sales tax and high import duties have earned Costa Rica the reputation as Central America's most expensive country. But by slightly modifying your life-style, buying national goods, riding the bus, shopping at local vegetable markets and taking full advantage of the country's excellent, low priced health care and insurance, a couple can live comfortably on about $1,200 per month.

**Factors considered:** Small home, $20,000; health insurance, $500/year; weekly fruits and vegetables, $10.00; health care, import duties, price of consumer items, utilities, food, gas, cars.

## Health (score: 8)

The safe drinking water here goes a long way toward improving the quality of life for everyone. Also, the country's excellent, low-cost medical care and dentistry enables residents to save thousands of dollars per year. Costa Rica has had great success in controlling dengue, malaria and cholera.

**Factors considered:** Emergency hospital visit, $21; potable water, quality of health care, diseases, infant mortality, number of physicians per capita.

## Living Environment (score 8)

This may be the most important factor for expatriates. Costa Rica's excellent climate, low rate of violent crime, quality education, good entertainment and cultural events, friendly people, and pro-U.S. attitude all combine to make the newcomer feel welcome.

**Factors considered:** Relatively safe, attitude of nationals, climate, bureaucracy, culture, education, obtaining residency, second passports, pensionado status, literacy rate, weather conditions.

## Stability (Score: 9)

Let's see, no army, a democratically elected government, freedom of religion, freedom of expression... the only reason this "Switzerland of the Americas" with its long history of individual liberty and freedom doesn't receive a perfect score is the degree of political corruption which occasionally provokes some civil unrest.

**Factors considered:** Civil liberties, political rights, corruption, democratically elected government, social guarantees.

**Business** (Score: 7)

Foreigners have the same rights as Costa Ricans regarding the ownership of businesses and real estate. The country's low labor costs, free trade zones and large middle class with disposable income have attracted the foreign investor. Negatives here are the bureaucracy, corruption and the "mañana syndrome."

**Factors considered:** Investment incentives, opportunities, real estate and corporate law, tax benefits, offshore corporations, telecommunications and internet.

## COSTA RICA

| Cost of Living | Health | Living Environment | Stability | Investing | Total Score | Utopia |
|---|---|---|---|---|---|---|
| 7 | 8 | 8 | 9 | 7 | 39 | 50 |

# 10 QUICK TIPS
## FOR THE NEWCOMER

The decision to move to a foreign country brings with it uncertainty, stress and even fear about adjusting to the new culture and customs. The following is a list of 10 answers to the questions most frequently asked by newcomers to Costa Rica.

1. A semi-decent looking car in average condition costs a minimum of $5,000 here, while a car in good condition could cost $10,000 or more. It's generally better to import a car from the U.S., even though the bureaucratic red tape, shipping arrangements and import duties cause the stress factor to rise. Importing a car isn't necessarily less expensive, but the vehicle -- unexposed to Costa Rica's bumpy roads -- will almost certainly be in better condition. Example: 1989 U.S. car ($5,000) + shipping ($1,000) + import taxes ($4,000) = $10,000.

2. Before deciding to move permanently to Costa Rica, it is vital to come beforehand for a minimum of six months to one year. The extended visit will expose you to the new culture and customs and help you determine if Tico life is for you.

3. Don't invest in anything without fully investigating and understanding what the investment is. There are more scams and bad business deals here than solid, profitable investments. Before investing, do a thorough background check on all elements of the project. It will save you money, trouble and heartache.

4. Learn Spanish. The happiest expatriates are those who assimilate their adopted country, mix in and enjoy. Learn-

ing a foreign language is very difficult. Enroll in a good Language school and dedicate yourself to learning.

Those who arrive with a good base of vocabulary and a thorough understanding of grammar will be speaking fluently after a year or two.

Learning the language "on the streets," without formal instruction, could take years. Many newcomers hire a full-time assistant for around $200.00 per month to show them around and help them with the language. This arrangement should be temporary.

5. Keep your expenses low your first years, until you know exactly how much you will need to live. If you adopt a Tico life-style, you can live on a minimum of $800.00 per month. Take buses and rent a small, "Tico" home for $300 to $400 per month. Check the La Nación newspaper's classified ads.

6. Bureaucracy and procrastination are alive and well in Costa Rica. Have patience with long lines and the tardiness of business meetings. Also be prepared for lots of car-horn honking and drivers who ignore traffic laws.

7. Payoffs are common in Latin countries. Don't be surprised if someone wants a little extra to get things done faster. The traffic police are notorious bribe accepters; for a quick ¢1,000 bill, many will let you off the hook.

8. This tip is for the guys. Women here are very attractive and friendly, but we caution you, like in business, to take your time, investigate and get to know the person well before getting seriously involved. Promiscuity is common here. A casual affair could get you in big trouble with someone's husband.

9. This tip is for the women. Be prepared for macho Tico cat calls and whistling from every male age group. This

custom has been around for years, and it's not going away. Promiscuity is common here. A casual affair could get you in big trouble with someone's wife.

10. Costa Rica is much safer than the U.S., but you need to use common sense. Don't become inebriated in public in San José; you'd be a favorite target for some mugger. Don't leave any personal item in plain view inside your parked car. Always lock your car, even if you're just doing a quick errand.

## ¡PURA VIDA!

*Bob trades in his 18-wheeler in Texas for his two-wheel ox-cart in Costa Rica.*

# GENERAL INFORMATION

## COST OF LIVING

Costa Rica already offers everything you need to live well and economically, but the "techies" and shopping fanatics among us will have to rethink their budgets and life-styles a bit in order to be happy here.

Brand name, top-quality clothing, imported U.S. munchies, semi-prepared packaged foods and most state-of-the-art electronics are either exorbitantly priced here, or are not available at all.

"Geez! Does that mean I can't buy that new cyber/java thingamajigger with an integrated microprocessor and 16 megs of RAM that can figure my tax return, send e-mail, feed the dog and brew a great cup of coffee?"

Probably not, but those who thrive on these and other products take advantage of their trips to the U.S. to buy and bring back the consumer goods they crave.

Locally produced foods and other products, as well as entertainment in general, is much less expensive in Costa Rica. A complete meal in a local restaurant will range from $2.00, in a low-cost café, to $15.00 for fine dining, including wine.

In an inexpensive "soda" or café, you can get a breakfast that includes two eggs, toast, rice and beans, orange juice, and coffee for roughly $2.00.

For a meal that includes steak, rice, beans, salad and a soft drink or a beer, you pay an average of $4.00, which can be less depending on the place.

## COMMON GROCERY PRICES

| | |
|---|---|
| Tuna (One can local brand) | $0.87 |
| Del Monte Canned Sliced Peaches | $1.70 |
| Kellogg's Corn Flakes (9.3 oz) | $1.88 |
| Oreo Cookies (lb) | $3.01 |
| Budweiser Beer (1can) | $0.93 |
| Domestic beer | $0.40 a bottle |
| Lays Potato Chips | $3.57 |
| Campbell's Chicken Noodle Soup | $1.63 |
| Loaf of bread | $1.17 |
| Bananas | $0.03 ea. |
| Pineapples | $0.85 each |
| Toilet paper | $1.19 (4 rolls) |
| Sirloin steak | $2.65 a pound |
| Soft drinks | $0.38 a bottle |
| Milk | $0.90 per gallon |
| Miami Herald International edition | $1.60 |
| Tico Times (English Weekly Newspaper) | $0.70 |
| Cosmopolitan Magazine | $3.85 |
| Time Magazine | $5.90 |

The secret to an economical lifestyle in Costa Rica is "imitate the locals." Locally grown produce and domestic meats and other nationally produced goods are economical and of a good quality. The box above should give you an idea about average prices for common grocery items.

On the other hand, cameras, watches, telephones, cars, and almost all imported, manufactured articles are usually double the U.S. price. Computer prices are relatively low because taxes on them are minimal, as a result of efforts to improve technology in the country.

Buying a car here is expensive, due to import taxes (see Import Car section). For example, a 1987 Nissan Pathfinder that costs $4,000 in the U.S., would probably set you back about $11,000 in Costa Rica.

But who needs a car, anyway? Costa Rica's excellent bus system economically connects almost every location in the country. Even an eight to 10-hour ride will cost less than $10.00, one way. In the San José metro area, bus fares average $0.10 to $0.25. If you get a taxi, you pay $0.58 for the first kilometer, $0.28 to $0.30 for each additional one (1.6 kilometers equal 1 mile).

Aside from made-to-order clothing, which is inexpensive here compared to other countries, apparel is costly, especially for certain brand names.

Homes cost about half what they do in the U.S. Prices range from $15,000 for a 3-bedroom, 1-bath home in a nice Costa Rican neighborhood, up to $50,000. In an upper-class neighborhood, a home with a good-size yard can be purchased for $100,000 to $200,000. Most homes do not come with appliances such as refrigerators and stoves.

Rental housing is moderately priced. A 2-bedroom house or apartment can be rented for about $300 to $400 a month and it may have some furniture. Rent in upper-class neighborhoods runs from $500 to $2,000 or more per month.

### A COSTA RICAN MONTHLY BUDGET FOR TWO PEOPLE

| | |
|---|---:|
| Rent (3 bd. rm. Costa Rican Home) | $ 350.00 |
| Housekeeper (5 days/week 4 hrs/day $1.45/hr.) | 116.00 |
| Food | 200.00 |
| Electricity | 23.00 |
| Water | 7.00 |
| Telephone (local calls) | 15.00 |
| Cable T.V. | 25.00 |
| Transportation (bus, taxi) | 30.00 |
| Health Insurance (couple over 40) | 90.00 |
| Miscellaneous | 100.00 |
| Entertainment (once a week) | 130.00 |
| **Total** | **$ 1086.00** |

Utilities are also inexpensive. Electricity averages $20 a month. Heating and air-conditioning are not necessary in the Central Valley. Your telephone bill with local calls average $15, cable T.V. with CNN and 40 other stations costs $25.00. Domestic workers (live-in maids and gardeners) are paid less than $200 a month. Local telephone calls cost $0.05.

The cost of living in Costa Rica is low by general standards, but it does not mean, in any sense, that life quality be lower than elsewhere. For $1,200 a month, two people can live comfortably, and for $2,000 a month, live in luxury.

## *SALARIES IN COSTA RICA*

The Costa Rican government establishes minimum salaries for all types of jobs, which must be observed by em-

| *COMMON SALARIES* | Colones | Dollars *<br>(approx.) |
|---|---|---|
| Maids | ₡25,637 | $119 |
| Farm hands | 40,392 | 188 |
| Store clerks | 40,392 | 188 |
| Non-qualified worker<br>(construction, etc.) | 35,184 | 164 |
| Qualified worker<br>(construction, etc.) | 38,975 | 182 |
| Bus drivers | 47,208 | 220 |
| Phone exchange operators | 51,698 | 241 |
| Secretaries | 51,698 | 241 |
| Computer operators | 62,060 | 290 |
| Private accountant | 74,122 | 346 |
| Professionals | 75,328 | 352 |
| Professionals (full time) | 100,899 | 471 |

\* *Depending on the rate of exchange.*
*Additionally, by the law, every worker is entitled to a bonus one-month salary at the end of the year.*

ployers. However, only unexperienced workers get the starting salary, since experience and training usually lead to better wages.

The current starting monthly wages were decreed in Oct. 1996. See the "Common Salaries" box on the previous page to get an idea about average pay for typical jobs.

## *WORKING FOR SALARY IN COSTA RICA*

Foreigners are not allowed to work for salary in Costa Rica, except when they become permanent residents or when, under special legal provisions, they are permitted to work to provide a specialized service not readily available.

Each company is permitted to hire a certain percentage of foreigners to work for them. The work permit must be renewed each year and is good for as long as you stay employed with the company. In this way, many foreigners work as tourist guides, English teachers and business consultants.

Under this provision, those people are normally first contracted overseas by a company or organization that has taken the previous steps with local authorities. The interested party overseas has to visit a Costa Rican consulate for the proper procedures to obtain a work permit.

For information in Costa Rica, contact Dirección General de Migración y Extranjería (220-1860) and Migraciones Laborales (223-1478). It is up to the employer to initiate the proper paperwork for the work permit.

Once you become a permanent resident, you may work in Costa Rica just as any country national. Except for the right to vote or to hold public office by popular election, a permanent resident enjoys the same rights as Costa Ricans (see Residency Section for more information).

According to Costa Rican law, foreigners without permanent residency may own and operate their own company, while supporting themselves from the business's proceeds. They may not however, earn an actual "salary," in the sense that one of their employees does.

## BUSINESS HOURS

Offices and stores generally open at 8:30 or 9:00 a.m., and may close for lunch from 12:00 noon to 2:00 p.m., then reopen until 5:00 or 6:00 in the evening. On Saturdays, many businesses may be open in the morning only.

## BUREAUCRACY

Having a sense of humor when living in Costa Rica may help alleviate inevitable frustrations that occur when dealing with the "system." Be prepared for long delays with business transactions that require paperwork such as processing insurance claims, obtaining health care, and drivers' licenses. Waiting in long lines at banks and at airport immigration counters is not unusual.

## CORRUPTION

Tourists aren't the only ones drawn by Costa Rica's climate, peace and proximity to the U.S. The country also attracts fugitives from justice and other undesirables fleeing responsibilities or obligations back home. Such infamous international crooks as U.S. financier Robert Vesco and alleged gun and drug runner for the contra revolutionary movement John Hull, enjoyed years of peaceful life here until the former was finally thrown out by then President Alberto Carrazo in 1978, and the latter fled the country to avoid murder charges.

Many of these criminals and alleged criminals enjoyed close relationships with top government officials. One of former President Oscar Arias' political appointees, Ricardo Alem, was convicted in 1995 of money laundering by a Costa Rican court and of international drug trafficking by a U.S. court in Miami. He is currently in jail there.

Even more dangerous for the newcomer or foreign resident are the plethora of shady characters, scamsters and swindlers who often come to Costa Rica to flee criminal charges in their own countries, or to avoid paying back taxes to the U.S. Internal Revenue Service (IRS). These characters prey on the innocence of the newcomer, "dazzling" him or her with their "incredible knowledge" of how to get things done here and then offer "once in a lifetime" business opportunities that only leave the innocent investor poorer and wiser.

We at OG books know of a handful of these swindlers that are operating *right now* in Costa Rica, but are skilled at covering their tracks and have never been indicted here. Don't fall victim to these swindlers! Always remember -- If a deal sounds too good to be true, it probably is.

## *PAY OFFS*

A popular misconception in Costa Rica is that anything can be accomplished by slipping a few bills under the counter to a key official or politician. This certainly does happen every day, but it often blows up in the face of the person offering the bribe.

Although tedious, time consuming and rife with bureaucracy, the country's procedures for acquiring building permits, liquor or gambling licenses, residency and a bevy of other authorizations are best obtained legally and legitimately.

We've often observed how "corner cutting" during one presidential administration comes back to haunt its author as the new administration, eager to enforce its public stance as "tough on corruption," makes an example of the case. Many of San José's bar owners are now facing this situation, as the city's new governor is strictly applying and enforcing rules that have been on the books for years but never applied.

As time consuming and ridiculous as a procedure seems, we highly recommend that newcomers shrug their shoulders, arm themselves with patience and make an extra effort to follow the rules. Not to do so could lead to economic disaster.

## POST OFFICE

Letters may be sent to an individual person in care of "Lista de Correos" (general delivery), Correo Central, 1000 San José (or the city or town where you are located). There is a small charge for each letter picked up.

When writing to hotels, people or businesses, use the post office box ("Apdo.") instead of the street address.

Theft is rampant among postal employees. Don't send anything valuable through the national mail service. Many businesses and individuals use one of the local mail forwarding service based in Miami.

Star Box, Tel: (506) 257-3443, Fax: (506) 223-5624, is a mail forwarding company that gives you access to all U.S. Postal Service and private courier benefits. The Costa Rica-based subscriber is assigned a post office box and street address in Miami. All incoming and outgoing mail is then channeled through the Miami address and forwarded daily to Costa Rica. Star Box is much safer and faster than its competition. The $9.50 minimum monthly rate is worth it.

## TELEPHONES

Public telephones, accept coins in ¢5, ¢10 and ¢20 denominations. Set the coin in the slot on top of the phone, then dial. The coin will drop down when the connection has been made. It is best to place another coin in the slot while talking, which will automatically drop down as needed. For telephone numbers not listed in the phone book, dial 113.

International calls may be made from public telephones either by calling collect, using your international calling card or using Costa Rica's new prepaid calling cards called "chip"cards or "Colibrí 197."

By the end of 1998, the telecommunications branch of the Costa Rican Electricity Institute (ICE) will install more phone lines to make the country the leader in Central America.

Purchasing a telephone line can be troublesome depending on where you live. In early 1994, Costa Rica changed from a six-digit numbering system to one of seven digits, in order to make available more lines. If lines are available in your area, it will take between two and four months for ICE to connect the service at your home at a cost of around $300.

Cellular telephone service has caught on in a big way in Costa Rica. Customers often complain of the device's limited range, but managers, lawyers, business owners and other professionals are rarely without one. Service costs around $20 per month for the first 60 minutes. After that, calls are charged at around $0.15 per minute.

The main ICE office is located on the North side of the Sabana Park, the phone number is 220-7720.

## *PAYMENT OF BILLS*

Telephone and electric bills may be paid at the I.C.E. offices at La Sabana, San Pedro, downtown San José (Avenida 2, Calle 1), or at any I.C.E. office in Costa Rica. Payment may also be made at some banks and local supermarkets, such as Mas x Menos, Periféricos and Yaohan's.

## *CURRENCY*

The official currency is the colon. Bills are in denominations of ¢50, ¢100, ¢500, ¢1,000, and ¢5,000, and coins in ¢1, ¢2, ¢5, ¢10, ¢20 and a new gold-colored ¢25.

New gold-colored coins are also in circulation now to replace the ¢100 and ¢50 bills.

The exchange rate floats in relation to the U.S. dollar. Dollars and other currencies can be exchanged at banks and at most large hotels. There are also money exchange brokers that are located throughout San José. It is not recommended to exchange money with people on the street for this can be very dangerous with many scams reported.

## LANGUAGE

Spanish is the national language, although many Costa Ricans speak English, particularly the business class in San José and in the Caribbean region among the Jamaican immigrants.

## BANKING (Also see Banking Section)

Banks and large hotels will exchange money. Checking accounts, debit cards and electronic teller machines are now available at all public and private banks. Most banks are open Monday through Friday from 9:00 a.m. to 3:00 p.m., with evening and weekend hours available at selected branches.

## TOURIST ENTRY AND EXIT

Visitors are granted 30 or 90-day tourist visas, depending on their country of origin. Citizens of the United States or Canada need only a tourist card, issued upon arrival, for an up to 90-day visit. Most other nationalities are required to present a passport and visa.

Thirty-day tourist visas can be extended for an additional 60 days. Ninety-day tourist visas cannot be extended, but if the traveler leaves Costa Rica for 72 hours and then re-enters, a new 90-day visa will be granted.

If you overstay your tourist visa, you may be subject to a fine of ₡350 ($1.90) per month, plus a ₡7,000 ($38) exit tax. You may also be required to purchase "Pensiones Alimenticias" stamps from the Court to prove that you are not leaving any children in the country. Tourists have five days to leave the country once they receive their exit visa. Most travel agencies can take care of these transactions for you.

When leaving the country, U.S. Customs allows an exemption of $400.00 per person in goods. Canadian residents may use a $300.00 exemption.

## HOLIDAYS

On national holidays all government offices, banks, post offices, and most private businesses and shops are closed. Many businesses close down for all of Semana Santa, or Easter week, and there is no bus service on Holy Thursday and Good Friday. Many offices are closed between Christmas and New Year's. The following box lists all the country's national holidays, only the ones that are starred required mandatory pay or days off for employees.

### COSTA RICAN HOLIDAYS

| | |
|---|---|
| Jan. 1 | New Year's Day* |
| Jan. 15 | Santa Cruz Fiestas |
| March 19 | St. Joseph's Day (San José) |
| March | Oxcart Driver Day (Día del Boyero) |
| Holy Week | Holy Thursday and Good Friday* |
| April 11 | Juan Santamaría's Day (local hero)* |
| April 21 | Pilgrimage in Cartago (Romería) |
| May 1 | Labor Day* |
| May | University Week |
| June | Father's Day (Third Sunday) |
| July 25 | Annexation of Guanacaste Province* |
| Aug. 2 | Virgin of Los Angeles Day |
| Aug. 15 | Mother's Day* |
| Sept. 15 | Independence Day* |
| Oct. 12 | Columbus Day - Discovery of America |
| Oct. 12 | Limón Carnaval |
| Oct. 31 | Halloween |
| Nov. 2 | All Souls Day |
| Dec. 8 | Immaculate Conception |
| Dec. 25 | Christmas Day* |

## NEWSPAPERS - MAGAZINES

There are several new and used bookstores in San José for reading material in English, German, and Spanish. New books in English tend to be rather expensive, but competition is on the rise, and prices are dropping.

English language newspapers, magazines and books are for sale all over the San José area. Some of the most popular bookstores include Librería Internacional, 400 meters west of Taco Bell, San Pedro; Book Traders, Ave. 1, Calles 3/5; Gambit, Ave. 3, Calle 35, Los Yoses; Harlequin, Plaza Los Colegios Shopping Center, Moravia; Librería Francesa, Ave. Central/1, Calle 3; Librería Lehman, Ave. Central, Calle 1/3 or Plaza Mayor, Rohrmoser; Librería Universal, Ave. Central, Calle Central/1, or southeast corner of La Sabana; Chispas Books, Ave 1 and Central, Calle 7; Staufer, Plaza del Sol Shopping Center, Curridabat.

Two local weekly newspapers printed in English are "The Tico Times" and "Costa Rica Today" (tourist tabloid). The International Edition of the Miami Herald, U.S.A. Today, and other, newspapers from abroad are also available.

**English Language Publications Available:**

| | |
|---|---|
| Barron's | Wall Street Journal |
| International Herald Tribune | Sporting News |
| Sports Illustrated | USA Today |
| Washington Post | Time Magazine |
| Newsweek Magazine | New York Times |

## HEALTH

Health care in Costa Rica is first-rate and highly affordable. Private medical or dental specialists charge between $15 and $30 per visit. Plastic surgery is also excellent.

Tap water is safe to drink almost anywhere you go in Costa Rica. In San Jose and its suburbs, the national Water and Sewer company (AyA) supplies the water. In low-lying areas, particularly at the beach and around banana plantations, it is wise to boil or otherwise purify water for drinking, ice, washing vegetables and brushing teeth.

Central America's tropical climate is a prime breeding place for a variety of diseases, but while dengue, malaria and cholera have reached epidemic proportions in other countries, Costa Rica has done an excellent job preventing their spread (see Health Care section for symptoms and prevention). AIDS is a problem here, as everywhere. Practice safe sex.

## UTILITIES

Electric current is 110 volts AC; the same as in the U.S.

## CLOTHING

Informal clothing is suitable for most events. It is recommended that one wear a dress or jacket and tie for formal occasions. Generally, lightweight clothing with a sweater for cool evenings and trips to the mountains is suggested. During the May to November wet season, an umbrella is a must.

## TRANSPORTATION

**Buses** Costa Rica has an excellent bus system. The main bus station is called the "Coca-Cola," located on Calle 16, between Avenidas 1 and 3. It used to be the site of the old Coca Cola bottling plant. Buses leave on a daily basis transporting people almost anywhere in the country. Most other bus stops are spread around the city. Bus fares in the San José metropolitan area range from $0.10 to $0.70. Most bus drivers can direct you to the correct stop.

**Taxis** When you need to go somewhere quickly or don't feel up to learning the bus system, a taxi is your best choice.

Thousands of the red cabs cruise the streets in search of fares, but Costa Rica also has a thriving population of illegal taxis or "piratas" that work out of their dilapidated vehicles.

Piratas usually charge less, but don't have the obligatory fare meter, called a "maría," to keep them honest.

All red or orange taxis have marías and are required by law to use them. At press time, taxi meters start marking at ¢125 ($0.58) for the first kilometer, with each additional kilometer costs ¢60. A fare increase is imminent, however. If you see the meter isn't running, politely say to the driver, "póngame la maría, por favor, " (please turn on the meter).

Outside the metro area, taxi fares are usually negotiated. Be sure to determine the price before getting in the cab. Ask a taxi driver or hotel clerk for assistance to your location.

**Car Rental and Air Travel** Car rental agencies are easily located in major cities. For a reasonable price a person can fly anywhere in the country on the local airlines SANSA or Travel Air.

## *NUMBERING OF STREETS*

San José streets are numbered using a logical grid system. The streets, or "calles," run north/south, while the avenues or "avenidas" run east/west.

The city is divided by *Avenida Central,* which becomes *Paseo Colon* west of Hospital San Juan de Dios, and *Calle Central.* Streets west of Calle Central are evenly numbered, while those east have odd numbers. Similarly, even-numbered avenues are situated south of Avenida Central, while odd-numbered avenues lie to the north.

The city's grid system is highly logical, but almost none of the intersections are marked with the corresponding street or avenue numbers. When giving directions, Ticos always uses prominent landmarks (see directions section), rather than streets and avenues.

**Abbreviations used for addresses in this guide are:**

|  |  |
|---|---|
| c | calle |
| av | avenida |

| | |
|---|---|
| m | meters |
| ctl | central |
| apdo | apartado (for mailing addresses) |

**Directions, Tico-style** Costa Ricans have a unique way of giving directions that may take a little getting used to. They almost never refer to San Jose streets and avenues, which aren't marked, anyway. Instead they will give directions from a known landmark and direct you east, west, north or south with the distance in meters. One block measuring 100 meters. Example: the Holiday Inn is located 300 meters north of the Plaza de la Cultura.

## *GREETINGS*

In Latin America when most people are first introduced they shake hands with each other. In Costa Rica it is customary for women to greet and say good-bye with a friendly kiss on the cheek. This is also true for men and women who have a friendly relationship. Children often greet their elders in the same manner.

### ¡PURA VIDA!

"Turn left where the old fig tree used to be. When you get to Manuel's market, go 300 meters south until you see an old blue pickup with a cracked windshield, don't turn there, just keep..."

## GIFTS

Gifts are given at birthdays, Christmas, weddings, anniversaries, showers, graduations, baptisms, first communions, births and farewells. Some stores have weddings lists.

## SOCIAL EVENTS

**Parties (Private and Informal)** Get accustomed to Tico time. It is customary for Ticos to arrive from one-half to two hours late. Don't expect your guests to arrive on time. Formal lunches may not begin until 3 or 4 p.m., teas until 5 or 6 p.m., and dinners until at 9 p.m. When entertaining, prepare a meal that can be easily heated when guests finally arrive.

## TIPPING

**Maids** Hotel maids are tipped at your discretion. Take into consideration the number of people in your party and the type of service you have received. Most people, if they are a house guest in a private home, will tip the maid if she performs a service for you, like laundry or other miscellaneous errands. Tip the maid again at your discretion, like ₡200 to ₡500.

**Waiters** A 10% service charge is always included in the bill at restaurants, hotels and clubs. If you wish to leave an extra tip, it is acceptable to do so. On a special holiday or occasion, at a restaurant or club, it is a good idea to tip your waiter in order to get speedy service.

**Parking Attendants** It is not common to tip parking attendants. Unless the attendant has performed a special service for you. When a young child offers to watch your car, it is best to say yes in order to secure the safety of your car. These attendants are usually in front of restaurants and theaters and expect a tip between ₡50 and ₡200.

**Store Clerks and Supermarket Boys** Store clerks are never tipped. Supermarket boys are tipped between ¢50 and ¢100 if they take packages to your car.

## DOMESTIC EMPLOYEES

**Contracts** (consult the Labor Code for specific laws) Most employers do not enter into a written contract with their domestic employee because both employee and employer are covered by the Labor Code. If you decide on a written contract you should observe certain requirements that can be found under Article 24 of the Labor Code.

**Salary** Part-time domestic help at the time of this writing, ranges from $1.80 to $2.00 per hour. With live-in full time help a minimum month's salary of ¢25,637 ($119.00) is required. Also a furnished room plus board is required.

**Hours** In Costa Rica the Labor Code allows a maximum 12-hour work day. It is common for employers to allow the domestic help time during the week to attend to banking, doctor appointments or other needed errands.

## BRINGING YOUR PETS

Yes! You can bring your pets into the country too. However, some procedures must be followed that involve paperwork, a small fee, and some patience.

The first requirement is a certification from a registered veterinarian stating that your pets are free of internal and external parasites. Your pet's vaccinations must be up-to-date against rabies, distemper, leptospirosis, hepatitis, and parvovirus. The rabies vaccination must not be older than three years. These documents must be certified by the Costa Rican consulate closest to your hometown.

Beware! Your pet can be refused entry, placed in quarantine, or even put to sleep if entry requirements are not met.

In any event, there is a 30-day grace period to straighten things out once you arrive here.

Additional information is available through the Depto. de Zoonosis, Ministerio de Salud, Apartado Postal 10123, San José, Costa Rica. Tel. (506) 223-0333, extension 331.

The Clínica Veterinaria, run by Dr. Adrián Molina in Escazú, will help you with all the necessary paperwork to bring your pet to Costa Rica, give him a call at 228-1909.

## ENJOYING CASINOS

Those who enjoy casinos have a wide variety from which to choose. Most are located in San José and in some beach resorts. Rules are slightly different here to those in the U.S. or in Europe, but gambling is no less fun the Tico way.

Most casinos serve free drinks while you play. Most operate from about 6 p.m. to 3 or 4 a.m. Popular hotels with casinos include San José Palacio, Camino Real, Cariari, Holiday Inn, Balmoral, Corobicí, Irazú, Presidente, Herradura, Gran Hotel, Flamingo and Fiesta, Puntarenas.

## CRIME IN COSTA RICA

Living in Costa Rica is much safer than living in any large city in North America or other parts of the world. The rate of violent crime is very low, but petty theft rises and falls with the country's gross domestic product.

In 1996, two high-profile kidnappings grabbed headlines. Both were carried out by impoverished former Nicaraguan contra rebels. Both crimes were committed for the payoff -- not for political means -- and were resolved peacefully. Police subsequently arrested the perpetrators and recovered almost all of the ransom money paid.

**Street Crime** Common sense is any foreigner's best defense against street crime.

When parking your car, be sure it is located in a secure place, locked and all valuable articles out of sight. You will notice that most stores and houses have bars on the windows and doors to prevent burglaries.

**Limón**  The Atlantic port town of Limon and the beaches south to the Panama border have had a streak of violent assaults this past year. Security has been greatly improved and neighbors have organized to quash crime, but it's still a good idea to be cautious when visiting the Atlantic coast.

**Chapulines**  Young purse and jewelry snatchers, popularly known as "chapulines," have become an increasing problem in San José. Often working in groups of three or more, these young delinquents carry knives or ice-picks and aren't shy about using them. When walking in San José, it's a good idea to remove expensive watches or jewelry, be discrete with any electronic goods, such as cameras or Walkmans, and avoid carrying large amounts of cash. Adept pickpockets abound.

**Scams**  A number of dishonest Americans, Canadians, Europeans and Costa Ricans thrive here and are waiting to take your money in real estate scams and other ingenious schemes. If an offer seems to good to be true, it usually is, so beware. If you have been assaulted or swindled, call 9-1-1 for emergency assistance in San José, or the police in rural areas.

**Police bribes**  Police are prohibited from asking for or accepting bribes for reduced traffic or other violations. Nevertheless, many find bribes an excellent means of increasing their meager incomes. It's usually best to refuse to pay the bribe and immediately solicit the officer's name and badge number. He is required to comply. Any dishonest act should be reported at once. Judicial Police (OIJ) Tel: 255-0122; Transit Police, Tel: 227-2188.

The key word is common sense! Most foreigners who have lived here for any length of time will tell you that common sense will prevent or greatly reduce anything happening to you or your property.

## SOCIAL LIFE

Speaking little or no Spanish is no reason to stop you from having an active social life. Two English newspapers (Tico Times and Costa Rica Today) publish weekly events and activities from Republicans and Democrats Abroad to club news and activities at the American Legion; these newspapers serve an important link to the foreign population.

**Sports** The sports buff won't miss a game at the many sports bars (mostly owned by foreigners) throughout San José such as Tiny's, Nashville South, Piano Blanco Bar or Mac's American Bar in Escazú.

**Nightlife** The night owl won't be lonely at the numerous restaurants, bars, disco's and small town dance halls located all over the country. Popular socializing and dance places are La Plaza Discotheque, El Cuartel, Río, Babúu, La Cantina and Las Tunas.

In Costa Rica prostitution is legal, and Key Largo and Happy Days are the places most frequented by ladies of the night. But be cautious. If you are invited to spend an evening with your lady friend, you might awaken to find yourself minus your wallet and other valuables.

After a night of dancing and meeting new friends, go to La Esmeralda, where you will find good food and famous mariachis that play until the sun comes up.

## RESTAURANTS – BARS – CANTINAS

The San Jose area has a wide variety of international restaurants, local typical food establishments and even fast food restaurants such as McDonalds, Burger King, Taco Bell, Kentucky Fried Chicken and Pizza Hut. At the many *soda* restaurants located throughout Costa Rica a complete meal that includes meat, rice, beans, plantains, salad and fruit drink cost between $2.00 and $3.00. In most bars and cantinas when a customer purchases an alcoholic drink they may receive a free *boca* (small plate of meat, chicken, sausage or other tasty munchie). Drinking establishments called cantinas are customarily for men only.

## SHOPPING

New malls, shopping centers and strip centers are springing up everywhere with such trendy shops as Liz Claiborne, Guess and ACA Joe. However, high import duties on these products often drive up the price. Most foreigners and wealthy Ticos head to Miami once or twice a year to bring back the clothing and other goods they crave.

Most newcomers to Costa Rica find the procedure for making a purchase in a department store a little baffling.

Once you've decided what you want to buy, the store clerk fills out an invoice, gives you a copy of it and directs you to the cash register or "caja." You must pay for the item and then present the validated copy of the invoice to a separate "packing" counter, where your merchandise will be waiting. This may seem a little complicated, but it's very effective in preventing theft.

Self service is catching on here, but is still not widespread, outside of supermarkets. Some hardware stores now feature self-service, and even small grocery markets are allowing customers down the aisles to help themselves.

**Major shopping Malls and Areas include** Mall San Pedro, which has become the metro area's three-story mecca for shopping fun and socializing, as well as Plaza Mayor (Rohrmoser), Trejos Monte Alegre (Escazu), Plaza Colonial (Escazu), Multiplaza (Escazu), Plaza del Sol (Curridabat), Plaza del Sur (Desamparados), Plaza Real Cariari (Heredia) and Mall Internacional Alajuela (Alajuela).

## SUPERMARKETS

There are a number of large supermarket chains in metropolitan San Jose similar to North American supermarkets but with the local brand names. A few supermarkets offer a good selection of North American imported food products, but at higher prices than back home.

Major supermarkets include Mas x Menos, Saretos, Perfericos, Pali and Automercado. Others, such as Yaohan and Muñoz y Nanne, cater to an upscale crowd, but sell imported foods and products that are hard to come by in other establishments.

All small towns and neighborhoods have a small grocery story or "pulpería," usually within easy walking distance, where area residents can conveniently purchase all the grocery essentials.

## MARRIAGE

Getting married in Costa Rica either by civil ceremony or by the church can be quite simple as long as you follow certain legal requirements. A civil ceremony can be done by a judge, attorney or notary. The majority of Costa Ricans are Catholic and are married in the Catholic church, which will impose additional requirements as well as the civil law requirements. Contact an attorney for more information.

## ADOPTION

The Costa Rican adoption agency is called the Nacional Child Welfare Agency *(Patronato Nacional de la Infancia)*. The approval process can take up to five months or longer. Once all the proper paper work has been submitted and approved the waiting period can take one-to-two years depending on the availability of children.

To qualify for an adoption, the petitioner must be at least 25 years of age and be at least 15 years older than the adopted child. When considering an international adoption it is important to fully understand the Costa Rican laws as well as the immigration and adoption requirements of your own country.

## SURNAMES

All Costa Ricans have two legal last names, their father's, which is always written first, and their mother's. For simplicity, the first last name is commonly used by itself, but all legal or formal documents contain both last names.

Women retain their original last names after marriage, but their children's last names are a combination of both the husband's and wife's. For example, if María Campos marries José Rojas, their children's last names will be Rojas Campos.

Some women choose to drop their second last name in favor of their husband's last name, but this is not common in Costa Rica.

**Courtesy Titles** It is a Latin custom when you want to show a sign of respect to the person you are addressing to use Don or Doña in front of the persons name. For example; Don Roberto or Doña Margarita.

### Movie Theaters in San José

| Theater | Address | Telephone |
| --- | --- | --- |
| Magaly | Barrio La California | 223-0085 |
| Omni | c. 3, a. Central/1 | 221-7903 |
| Colón | Paseo Colón, c. 38 | 221-4517 |
| Variedades | a. Central, c. 5 | 222-6108 |
| Colonial | Plaza Colonial in Escazú | 289-9000 |
| California | c.23, a.c1 | 221-4738 |
| Capri | a. Central, c. 9/11 | 223-0264 |
| Metropolitan | c.28, a. Central | 221-1219 |
| Universal | Paseo Colón, c. 26/28 | 221-5241 |
| Rex | a. 4, c. Central/2 | 221-0041 |
| Bellavista | a. Central, c. 17/19 | 221-0909 |
| Sala Garbo | a. 2, c. 28 | 222-1034 |
| Laurence Oliver | a. 2, c. 28 | 223-1960 |
| Mall San Pedro | San Pedro Rotunda | |
| Real Cariari | General Cañas Fwy. | |

## TELEVISION/CABLE

You will feel like you're back at home when watching the variety of English television channels available with satellite cable. The three U.S. networks ABC, CBS and NBC as well as HBO, C-SPAN, ESPN, MTV, Discovery and others are available. National programming is almost exclusively in Spanish, while cable offerings are similar to the U.S. Many English-language movies on cable are subtitled in Spanish.

The cost to subscribe averages $25.00 a month, or you can buy your own satellite dish. To order call:

| | | | |
|---|---|---|---|
| Super Canal | 231-2811 | Cable Tica | 254-8858 |
| Cable Color | 231-2811 | TV satellite | 226-6918 |
| Cable America | 238-1756 | | |

## THEATERS

The San Jose metropolitan area has more than 20 movie theaters that show recently released films from the United States in English with Spanish subtitles. Tickets average $2.00

## ACTIVITIES AND CLUBS

Costa Rica has a number of excellent private clubs and public facilities to keep people of all ages active. Many offer golf, tennis, bowling, gym, health spa, basketball, swimming and much more. Below list some of the private clubs in Costa Rica:

**Cariari Country Club** Offers an 18-hole golf course, six indoor and five outdoor tennis courts, swimming pool and gym facilities. Membership runs around $11,500 for the initial fee and a $37.00 monthly fee. Telephone 293-3211.

**Costa Rica Country Club** Considered Costa Rica's most exclusive, the club offers six outdoor and three indoor tennis courts and a nine-hole golf course. You must live in Costa Rica a minimum of two years before your application is considered. Shares when available cost around $15,000, with an entrance fee of $2,900 and monthly fee $50.00. Telephone 228-9333.

**Costa Rica Tennis Club** Features 11 tennis courts, gym, spa, bowling, two swimming pools, dinning area and bar. The cost to join is approximately $4,650, plus the monthly fee $40.00. Telephone 232-1266.

**The Spa Corobici** Offers gym, spa, sauna and snack shop. The cost to join is $47.00, plus a $35.00 monthly fee. Telephone 231-5533.

**The American Legion Club** Located in Escazú and situated on five acres, American Legion Post 10 is always active with a daily open bar, Sunday dancing and holiday fiestas. They also have a tennis court. Membership is around $100 for use of the club and tennis court. Telephone 228-1740.

**Club Olimpico** Offers a well-equipped gym, sauna, racquet ball court, massage therapy, Taekwon-do and much more. Membership costs $35.00 to join and $35.00 a month. Telephone 224-3560.

**The Indoor Club in Curridabat** Has four indoor and four outdoor tennis courts, basketball and volleyball courts, bowling and a weightlifting area. Membership is approximately $3,500 with a monthly fee of $25.00. Telephone 225-9344.

**Bello Horizonte Country Club** Offers two new tennis courts, a swimming pool and restaurant. To join you have to purchase a share for $150.00 and pay a one-time fee of $233, plus a monthly fee of $21.00. One membership entitles an entire extended family to use the facilities. Telephone 228-0924.

**La Sabana Park** - San José's premier park and center of weekend outdoor activity. The park extends nearly 40 hectares and offers three tennis courts, several basketball and volleyball courts, baseball diamonds, running track, bike paths, many soccer fields, picnic tables, two lakes and ducks. Membership: FREE!

## BETTER BUSINESS BUREAU

Without the benefit of experience, the newcomer's dilemma is always the same: Who to trust? The Better Business Bureau (BBB) of Costa Rica was formed in 1994 to put consumers in touch with trustworthy businesses. Contact the BBB at Tel/Fax: 257-5978 or 233-5785.

## RELIGION

Costa Rica is predominantly Catholic, but freedom of religion is a staple of society. The following offer services in English: B'Nai Israel, 225-8561, 232-9626; Chabad Lubavitch, 231-5745; National Bahaí Faith Information Center, 222-5335; Roman Catholic, 289-7530; San José Quakers, 233-6168; Episcopal Church of the Good Shepherd, 222-1560, Fax: 253-8331; Escazú Christian Fellowship, 228-0594; International Baptist Church, 225-4885; International Chapel of Saint Mary, 239-6709; Union Church, 235-6709; Unity, Tel/Fax: 228-6051; Victory Christian center, 282-7720; Jehovah's Witnesses, 293-2943, 221-1436.

## DUTY FREE ZONE

The South Pacific town of Golfito is a "duty-free zone" where everything from electronics to major appliances are sold free of prohibitive import duties. Residents find shopping at this *depósito libre* much easier than importing their goods from the U.S., even at the slightly higher prices.

## DRIVING

Valid foreign drivers licenses are honored in Costa Rica, as long as the license holder's tourist visa is still current. Tourists caught driving with an expired visa will be ticketed. Only residents can obtain a Costa Rican drivers license. For more information see Drivers License chapter.

## RADIO STATIONS

Several of the country's radio stations broadcast in English and provide information on tourist attractions, local living, events, sports, news and music. These stations are popular with Costa Rica's large foreign population and Ticos who enjoy pop and rock in English.

Radio Dos, 99.5 FM, features a 6 a.m. to 9 a.m. "Good Morning San José" show Monday through Friday. Super Radio, 102.3 FM offers a show of its own called "Breakfast in America," from 7:20 a.m. to 11 a.m. The new kid on the block is Radio Paladín, 107.5 FM, which is capturing audiences with a unique blend of musical genres, good bilingual DJ's and European flair.

# LIFE AS AN EXPATRIATE

Waxing poetic, we at OG books say life cannot be described; it must be *lived*. But the following gem of a letter that we discovered in the local English language newspaper The Tico Times comes about as close as anything we've ever read to depicting the joys and pitfalls of life in Costa Rica.

We've never met the author, J.A. Sinor, but congratulate him for so eloquently expressing what we all feel. We hope you enjoy it.

**Dear Tico Times:**

For those of you who may be on your way to visit Costa Rica, these are a few of the things you will find when you get here. Most of us living here already know all of this, but perhaps some of us have never really thought about all of it at the same time.

Costa Rica is a place where you will find that. . . Costa Ricans call themselves Ticos. . . all the taxi-cabs are red, except for the orange ones used at the airport. . . the bus drivers put Mercedes Benz symbols on the fronts of their buses regardless of their make (must be a status symbol). . . active volcanoes are a must to see, especially Arenal erupting at night. . . this is a real birdwatcher's paradise. . . some of the biggest potholes south of Chicago can be found here.

You can expect to see tens of chairs bolted in bank waiting rooms for those patient customers who spend hours waiting to cash their payroll checks. . . Il Ponte Vecchio in San

Pedro just won an award for one of the top 100 restaurants in Central America and serves the best Italian food you will ever taste, tell Tony I sent you. . . Juan Valdez really does drink Costa Rican coffee. . . it can take more than two years to get a license tag for your car, so relax and put that paper in your window and don't worry.

There is no Army. . . soccer is played with a passion almost every Sunday in every town throughout the country. . . all the children in school wear uniforms. . . you cannot do business without a lawyer, so don't even try it. . . there is a dental clinic and a bar on almost every corner. . . most motorists do not respect the traffic laws. . . people still say "good morning," "please," & "thank you". . . practically all motorcyclists wear helmets. . . whatever you plant in the ground will grow. . . the only two real weather forecasts are sunshine or rain.

**Blowing** your horn really doesn't get anyone's attention. . . only 16 percent of the population smokes. . . you should stay clear of buses on the road. . . in San José you don't need an air-conditioned home. . .Ticos prescribe medicine to each other. . . most of the time you can usually get directions if you are lost. . . the airport is now too small to handle the increase in tourism.

When you go to the movie theater, don't hold onto your ticket expecting the doorman to tear it in half and leave you with half — they want it all. . . at Christmas most all stores stock up & sell toys and roadside stands sell grapes and apples. . . anybody you see on the street with a stick considers himself a guard, and you will have to pay him to watch your car if you park.

You can really get sunburned unknowingly. . . when you go through customs, a green light means no one will open your bags. . . you could be days standing in line at the Immigration Office if you go without a good lawyer. . . traffic jams, once unheard of, are now everyday occurrences in San José. . . people love to watch airplanes land & take off.

**The** beer in Costa Rica is great, and the national favorite is Imperial. . . you should definitely buy your liquor in the airport at the duty-free store, since its prices are too good to be true. . . the best cut of beef anywhere is lomito. . . being late for an appointment is accepted and "no problema". . . a great variety of fruits and vegetables is available. . . you will never have to pump your own gas.

Marlene truly bakes the best birthday cake in Tibas at Choza Dulce...Costa Rica has beautiful mountains and breathtaking valleys. . . this is a culture which is very family oriented. . . you will see five-year-old cars that look new. . . all the homes and businesses have bars on their windows. . . only in Costa Rica does the straw in your Coke cup at the movies pop up like a submarine surfacing, and this phenomenon, I believe, might have something to do with the Equator?. . . the best view of the Central Valley at night is from the Hotel Tara in Escazú.

Mariachis will serenade your neighbors in the middle of the night when you least want to hear them. . . Ticos do exercise their right to vote, and celebrate election time as if it were Mardi Gras. . . the citizens are proud of their democracy. . .

**¡PURA VIDA!**

Just a quiet walk, down a San José street.

investments in teak farms and macadamia could put you in the poorhouse. . . at dinner parties you might not eat until after 11:00 p.m. . . .in Costa Rica business comes after socializing. . . you can eat lemons that are sweet and are called "limón dulce."

**It** can take more than a year to get a phone line installed. . . it used to be cheap for foreigners to live here, but not any more. . . there are no mail boxes and few street signs. . . you can count on beautiful weather December through April. . . you will see bougainvillea in six colors and long-stem roses can be bought really cheap. . . people paint their driveways green and their roofs red. . . there is great fresh-baked bread in bakeries everywhere.

You shouldn't believe your travel agent if he tells you most Costa Ricans speak English. . . it's not wise to change money on the street. . . what they sell in the stores called "natilla" is not really sour cream. . . some of the best cheeses are Monte Rico brand and make sure you try the chile jelly. . . a good cheap mango is hard to find. . . you can experience earthquakes and plenty of tremors if you decide to live here. . . the horses seem to be really skinny. . . most workers take pride in their work. . . it almost always gets dark at 6 pm. . . when it hits 60 degrees Fahrenheit, Ticos say it is cold!!! The Chicago Bulls is the favorite basketball team. . . you can find good medical care. . . the average dog is ugly. . . if the U.S. sneezes, Costa Rica will catch a cold. . . Pops ice cream is better than cookies and cream from Blue Bell in Texas. . . if you are looking for the U.S. Embassy, many people will send you to the ambassador's residence by mistake.

**Someone** decided that it would help all concerned to have the traffic lights blink green before turning yellow. . . at any time, anywhere, for any reason, you can hear fireworks in the sky. . . Ticos like to say *"Pura Vida"*. . . the word *"ahorita"* doesn't mean right now, but *"ya"* does . . .if you are looking for a great gift, Barry Biesanz Woodworks in Escazú has exquisite wooden boxes, etc.

Ticos are superstitious and claim that if your child has the hiccups, you can cure them by taping a thread on their forehead. . . some of the most beautiful sunsets can be seen at the beaches of Guanacaste. . . the cure-all for most illnesses is "an injection". . . the Ticos are early to rise, starting their day at 5:30 a.m. . . .the power goes out a lot for short periods of time. . . you should not try to walk between two cops hitting the beat in downtown San José. . . everybody has ants in their house. . . you will have to buy at least four new tires every year. . . for some reason you tend to end up with tons of coins at the end of each week.

And lastly, Costa Rica is not an island in the Caribbean.

J.A. SINOR, San José

# REAL ESTATE

The receptiveness of the host country is an important consideration for the overseas investor. As foreigners continue to "gobble up" prime real estate, prices rise and growing numbers of country nationals find they no longer have access, economically, to land that had once been in their families for generations.

Costa Rica is still an extraordinarily open and friendly nation that continues to welcome the foreign investor. Ticos are no longer as tolerant, however, of the "omnipotent" foreign landholder, who demonstrates little interest or understanding of the community, its people and its culture -- all the more reason for the newcomer to make extra efforts to learn Spanish and get to know the neighbors. That is, after all, what it's all about!

Property values have been steadily rising over the past ten years. Beach areas have tended to grow faster due to extremely high tourist potential. The Arenal area has seen a dramatic increase in values, because the beautiful lake/reservoir offers great fishing and sporting possibilities in a natural jungle setting.

Costa Rican tourism is still on the rise, with more than 800,000 visitors expected in 1996. Tourists are seeking new areas to visit, giving places once thought too remote or out-of-the-way, an economic and ecological boost. This will inevitably drive prices up. Past growth, and the obvious future growth in Costa Rica, mean that the real estate investor has and will continue to have an excellent resale market, not only in terms of the price, but also the availability of qualified buyers.

The nation is divided into seven provinces: San José, Alajuela, Cartago, Heredia, Guanacaste, Puntarenas, and Limón. The first four are landlocked, while Guanacaste and Puntarenas enjoy the warmth of the tropical Pacific, and Limón the warmth of the Caribbean. The three are well known by their many beaches of unsurpassed beauty.

## *The Seven Provinces*

**San José** The capital city, has a population of some 300,000 and boasts all modern amenities common to major cities. Foreigners often choose to live on San José's west side in communities such as Rohrmoser, Escazú and Santa Ana. Homes there are spaced farther apart, with neatly clipped lawns and a country feel.

The area is a stone's throw from downtown San José and has easy access to public transportation, cable television, utilities, fine restaurants, bilingual schools, shopping centers, medical facilities and more.

**Alajuela** Only 15 miles northwest of San José, Alajuela is Costa Rica's second largest city. The Juan Santamaría International Airport is located near here, and many prefer the climate, which is decidedly warmer than in the capital.

**Cartago** Once the country's colonial capital, Cartago is located 15 miles east of San José. A growing city, where quiet neighborhoods and green, cultivated fields contrast with modern industrial areas, Cartago is home to the country's only basilica, dedicated to the Virgin of Los Angeles, Costa Rica's patron saint.

**Heredia** This community, nicknamed the city of flowers, lies six miles north of San José. Some of the best views of the Central Valley can be had from the Heredia hills.

Many foreigners have settled in these cool, picturesque hills, which in spite of their rural feel, are only about 20 minutes from downtown San José

**Guanacaste** Unlike Costa Rica's other six provinces, the largest city in the northwest province of Guanacaste doesn't share the same name. Liberia, located about 150 miles northwest of San José is widely considered this province's principal city, with a hot dry climate and rural small town atmosphere.

**Puntarenas** The Pacific port city of Puntarenas is now largely dedicated to tourism, since the port facility was transferred to nearby Caldera. Puntarenas is a small, colorful town located about 60 miles west of the capital and is an easy beach day-trip from any Central Valley location.

**Limón** The Atlantic port city of Limón is rich in Afro-Caribbean culture. Many of the locals, descended from Jamaicans, speak English, or their own unique blend of Spanish and English. Located 100 miles from San José, Limón isn't a popular living community for foreigners, who prefer life in the beautiful Caribbean beach towns of Cahuita, Puerto Viejo or Punta Uva, but is the center for regional shopping and commerce.

## *CENTRAL VALLEY HOT SPOTS*

The Central Valley is the economic, cultural and business heart of Costa Rica. Most foreign residents settle here to take advantage of the proximity to San José, as well as modern shopping centers, restaurants, good schools and easier access to the rest of the country. Most prices listed are for middle to upper class properties. It is possible to find comfortable and secure housing in nice Tico neighborhoods for $18,000 to $30,000 in these areas. Rentals run from $250 to $400 per month.

## Alajuela

A bustling city in its own right, Alajuela offers movies, restaurants, bars, nightclubs and San José's arch-rival soccer team. It is attractive to foreigners because it has everything they need in a smaller town setting. Alajuela is a growing industrial center because of its proximity to the airport, but its quiet, rolling hills afford ideal living conditions.

Homes are priced $18,000 to $300,000. Land starts at $5.00 per square meter. Rentals from $250 to $2,000 per month.

## Cariari

Cariari or "Ciudad Cariari," as it is sometimes known, is one of the country's most exclusive living communities. A championship golf course is the centerpiece of the Cariari Country Club, which is surrounded by luxury homes and lots, that complement the Cariari Hotel and the Herradura Hotel and Conference Center.

The club features tennis, swimming, gym facilities, bars, and more. The community has its own on-site shopping center, while the new Real Cariari mall and movie theater is right across the freeway. Cariari is located some 20 minutes northwest of San José. Homes are priced $100,000 to $500,000. Land starts at $50 per square meter. Rentals from $700 to $3,000 per month.

## Escazú

Residents will tell you that there's nothing quite like Escazú, where a palatial estate may share a block with a bevy of humble, wood-plank or adobe homes, cows, chickens, horses and crops. Its proximity to San José -- only five minutes to downtown -- friendly atmosphere, green hills and spectacular views of the Central Valley have made it a favorite with foreign residents.

The town has restaurants, nightclubs, upscale shopping, discos, and more. For sports enthusiasts, there are a number of gyms and the famous Costa Rica Country Club, where the international tennis tournament *La Copa del Café* is played every year.

Bilingual schools and churches have sprung up to cater to the community's large foreign population, many of whom work at the U.S. Embassy in nearby Pavas. Homes of a style and quality to suit the foreign buyer are from $80,000 to $500,000. Land prices vary greatly, from $10 to $125 per square meter. Rentals from $400 to $3,000 per month.

### *La Garita/Atenas/Orotina*

A corridor that connects San José to the Pacific coast is another popular and picturesque place to live. La Garita, Atenas and Orotina are the major cities along this route that boast restaurants, hotels, and small-scale tourist activities. The main attraction for foreigners, however, is the climate, which is said by some to be the best in the world: a year-round average of about 72° Fahrenheit.

This is mostly farm country with some industry taking hold closer to the city of Alajuela. Residents shop in nearby Sarchí and Alajuela.

Orotina is about one hour from San José, while Atenas is about 45 minutes away, and La Garita is 35 minutes. This zone is expected to become more tourist and residentially oriented in the future, when the Ciudad Colón highway to Orotina is completed in about five years. Homes in this region are situated on large, half-to-10-acre lots, known as *quintas*. Prices range from $25,000 to $500,000. Land costs $2.00 to $10.00 per square meter. Rentals from $250 to $1,500.

### *Sabana/Rohrmoser*

La Sabana is San José's premier urban park, located at the west end of Paseo Colón. On the north and south sides of the park are Sabana North and Sabana Sur, and on the west side is the area known as Rohrmoser. All are upscale favorites with Ticos as well as foreigners. The people who live in these areas are middle to upper class Ticos and foreigners.

A number of restaurants, bars and discos provide entertainment close-to-home. The shopping at Centro Colón, Yaohan and Plaza Mayor, is among the country's most exclusive. Activities include movies at the Centro Colón, sports at La Sabana, several health clubs/gyms, squash and the Costa Rica Tennis Club. Downtown San José is five minutes away.

The Sabana/Rohrmoser area is expected to continue to grow as an upscale home/commercial/hotel district. Homes cost between $75,000 and $500,000. Land starts at $60 per square meter. Rentals from $300 to $2,000 per month.

### San Pedro/Los Yoses

These two districts have sprung up around the University of Costa Rica and its 40,000 students. The area is youth-oriented and urban, with the highest concentration of bars, restaurants, discos and other assorted night spots in San José.

Shopping and upscale living are among the city's best here. The new San Pedro Mall features 14 acres of shopping under one roof and prime people-watching vantage points.

Los Yoses is home to the North American-Costa Rican Cultural Center, referred to as simply the *Centro Culteral*. It is considered one of the country's best language schools and also hosts the English-language Mark Twain Library. The area boasts a number of smaller language schools, including the K-12, International Christian School.

Downtown San José is a mere five minutes away. Homes in the area range in price from $90,000 to $500,000. Land, from $70 to $90 per square meter. Rentals are anywhere from $200 (student living) to $2,500 per month.

### San Rafael de Heredia

San Rafael is set in the hills above the city of Heredia and is the hub of a larger area that encompasses the homes and homesites around the Castillo Country Club. The area is generally residential, mixing average Tico homes with mid-to-upscale foreign-style residences, but there are several hotels, restaurants, and lodges.

These green hills are a favorite with foreign and national tourists and picnickers. The climate here is considerably cooler, and large stands of pine and deciduous trees flourish. The nearest shopping is in the city of Heredia, most famous to foreigners as the birthplace of ex-president and 1987 Nobel Peace Prize winner Oscar Arias. In the future, the San Rafael area is expected to grow as a residential zone, with a smattering of tourism. San José is about 35 minutes away. Homes for the foreign buyer cost between $50,000 and $500,000. Land ranges from $10 to $35 per square meter. Rentals in the area run from $200 to $1,500 per month.

### Santa Ana/Ciudad Colón

Santa Ana/Ciudad Colón is the farthest western suburban area of San José. A lively mixture of Ticos and foreigners live here. Major shopping is available at Santa Ana 2000, as well as at the Multi Plaza mall, which features more than 60 stores, a food court and a Camino Real Hotel. Santa Ana and Ciudad Colón have less commercial activity and could almost be considered 'bedroom' communities. Ciudad Colón is twenty minutes from San José; Santa Ana, fifteen minutes. Mid-to-upscale homes range from $60,000 to $500,000. Land prices start at $12.00 per square meter. Rentals are from $250 to $1,500 per month.

## SPECULATING IN REAL ESTATE

Speculating in both improved and unimproved real estate is continuing to increase at a rapid pace. Hotels, bed and breakfasts and *cabinas* in the Central Valley and at the beaches have almost reached the saturation point.

Speculation has been especially active on both coasts, where in the last year or two the same parcel has been sold, then resold at double the price within the same month. There is no apparent reason driving this demand other than the fact that Costa Rica is currently a "hot spot" destination, and it seems everyone wants a piece of "paradise." It is obvious that the values of beach property are fueled by the amount of tourism coming to Costa Rica, which could result in highly inflated prices. It is also important to remember that there has not been much improvement to the infrastructure, i.e. roads, sewer, telephone and shopping facilities in the last five years to justify rapid appreciation.

What happens when the force behind land values at the beach slows down? There are signs that increased crime, higher vacation costs and overdeveloped tourist facilities could result in slower appreciation of property along the coasts. However, this is mainly directed at large, unimproved raw land parcels that have no access to water, electricity or telephone. Improved lots with all utilities, and well-constructed condominiums should continue to increase at a steady pace.

With tourism apparently slowing down, many real estate experts who used to point to the coastal properties as the best investments are now looking at real estate in the Central Valley.

They believe that property in the San José metropolitan area will continue to grow at a solid pace. The risky tourism trends that greatly affect the values of beach property won't have much influence in the metro areas. The entire metro area has dependable transportation and communication systems, good restaurants, shopping centers, theaters and medical services. It is the financial center of the country, and one-third of the population lives there.

The metropolitan area is surrounded by mountain ranges to the north, east and south. Because of these restrictions, the growth of this area is moving the only way it can: west. In the last four years, property in the western towns of Escazú and Santa Ana have increased 20 to 30 percent.

The growth west is fueled by the lack of suitable, well-priced properties close to San José, as well as the basic desire of Costa Ricans and foreigners to live away from the capital city's increased smog and traffic. High demand due to regionally superior climate and improved infrastructure also contribute.

The experts say both residential and commercially zoned land has good potential to increase in value, but they specifically point to the shortage of more than 150,000 homes. The following factors have contributed to the housing shortage:

1. The pent-up demand from the last 10 years, due to the lack of capital to create new infrastructure (roads, sewers, waterlines, etc.) and to upgrade the existing obsolete systems.
2. The substantial increase in tourism has attracted foreigners to live and invest in Costa Rica.
3. Approximately 65 percent of the population is under 30, which will increase the demand for housing now and well into the future.
4. Local municipalities lack plans for future subdivisions. With one year to plan and obtain permits and one year to construct, we will see two to three years of strong demand for residential lots and homes.
5. Within five years, the Ciudad Colón to Orotina Highway will be completed which will make the drive from San José to the Pacific Beaches a short 45 minutes. This highway will open up many properties west of San José thought too difficult to access before.

When affordable residential lots become available, buyers aggressively purchase them to build on now, or hold as an investment. The strongest demand is for lots priced from $7,000 to $12,000, which allows for a $20,000 to $30,000 home, priced for the middle-class Costa Rican. There is also a strong demand for upper-middle-class properties, with lots starting at $20,000 to $50,000 and homes ranging $50,000 to $100,000.

## *TIPS FOR A GOOD BUY*

When purchasing real estate in Costa Rica, or in any other foreign country, it is important to fully understand all the laws and government requirements to buy and build.

Your first step should be to choose a lawyer who comes highly recommended by organizations such as the American Chamber of Commerce or the U.S. Embassy. Never rely on professionals recommended by the seller of the property. Here are a few tips for the potential buyer:

**1. Send a Tico**

When researching areas or prices, send a Costa Rican friend to ask questions and inquire about prices. Pay a dependable, bilingual Tico if necessary. Often, if the seller thinks he or she is dealing with a Tico, the price offered will be closer to the range of a typically more modest national salary.

**2. Don't rely on the National Registry**

Assessed land values in the National Registry are never accurate. If you're interested in purchasing land or a home in a specific area, go there and knock on doors (or send a Tico to do it for you). Find out the going prices on real estate in the area that was recently sold. This will give you a good idea about what you should offer.

**3. Don't rely on advertisements**

Again, personal research is very important to be ensured the best land for the best price. Ticos don't advertise much. Go to your area of interest and ask around. Visit the local *pulpería* or small grocery store. Those who frequent these stores will know if anyone in town is considering selling. Talk to as many people as you can before you finally make an offer. The more information you have about an area or particular property, the better you'll be able to haggle.

**4. Expect to haggle**

Ticos love to haggle. Many times the land up for sale has been in their families for generations. Never be in a hurry when it comes to real estate. Make an offer and wait a while. If the land still hasn't been sold, make another offer. If the owner really wants to sell, he or she will be willing to negotiate.

**5. Negotiate in colones, not dollars**

If possible, do all negotiating and draw up all contracts in colones, the national currency. Sometimes you can ask the seller to give you a fixed amount of time to pay for the land. If you set the sale price in colones, you'll come out ahead over time as the colón continues to devalue.

Be aware of the local labor laws. In some cases, all employees of the previous owner, including maids, gardeners and caretakers, become the responsibility of the new owner. The new owner could also be liable for fines or back wages. Also, telephone lines are often hard to come by in Costa Rica, so its best to negotiate the purchase of the phone line with the house.

## *OWNERSHIP OF LAND*

Costa Rica's laws and Constitution protect private ownership of land, and foreigners enjoy the same rights as citizens. There are almost no restrictions to ownership of private land, except that given or sold to Costa Rican citizens as part of government programs, which can be freely traded or acquired by foreigners only after the original owner has held it for a certain period of time. Neither citizenship nor residence, nor even presence in the country, is required for land ownership.

## *REGISTRATION*

Costa Rica boasts a relatively safe form of title registration, centered in the National Property Registry or *Registro Nacional de Propiedad.*

Titles and plot maps are on file here, and changes in the property's status are recorded, making it easy to verify ownership of a property.

Before closing the deal, a dependable lawyer should conduct a thorough title search to establish the property's legal owner and to ensure it is without liens.

Once a deal is completed, you should also secure documents from your lawyer to prove that the sale was registered. This will prevent the previous owner from reselling the property to somebody else.

Just as anywhere else, Costa Rica is not without scamsters, both local and foreign, so it is wise to know who you are dealing with and to follow all procedures properly.

## FINANCING

Practically no local financing at economically feasible rates is available for property purchases. This is the result of high yields and rapid increase in property value, due to a growing population. However, the country's stability and security continue to make it attractive to the foreign investor.

## EARNEST MONEY

Making earnest money deposits and settling balances are fairly complicated procedures. Local bank trust departments can take care of these matters, but their procedures are ponderous and often inconvenient. Foreign banks are not yet allowed to provide this service. It is advisable to make deposits through a lawyer or agent, but only if the person is well-known and fully trusted.

## ZONING

Lawyers agree that zoning regulations in Costa Rica are reasonable and logical, although far less stringent than in countries such as the United States. All building and subdivision plans must be signed by a registered local engineer and they also require approval by the local municipality, the Ministry of Health, and the government Housing Department.

The permit process is slow-going, but patience and perseverance, rather than under-the-table payoffs, are always your best strategies.

## BROKERS

Only a limited number of brokerage companies and individuals have good reputations as serious professionals in Costa Rica. The Ministry of Economy issues real estate "certificates" on recommendations from the Chamber of Real Estate Brokers, which is dedicated to raising standards of both competence and ethics. However, the standards here are not as high as in North America, and the penalties are almost nonexistent. Be on the lookout for unscrupulous agents. If you're not comfortable with the agent, it's best to go directly to the seller. The Remax AsFisa real estate company comes highly recommended by past clients. This franchise is co-owned by a Canadian and a Tico with years of professional experience. Give them a call at (506) 290-3183, or fax, (506) 296-4358.

## TAXES

The taxes paid on properties in Costa Rica are very low. Yearly property taxes vary from 0.5 percent to 1.5 percent of the declared value of the property. This declared value, in common law practice, is much lower than the actual value.

## CLOSING COSTS

Closing costs include a transfer land tax, a stamp tax, and legal fees. Closing costs typically run 5 percent to 6 percent of the sale price and are usually split 50/50 between buyer and seller. The transfer and land taxes are assessed based on the declared value, while legal fees are charged based on the **sale price** of the property.

## DEVALUATION

The colón has been devaluing at a rate of around 15 percent per year. Economists estimate that it should be at 250 colones to the dollar by the end of 1997.

It is important to fully understand how the devaluation of the colón can affect your return on investment. This is called dual currency economics.

Currency exchange is a significant factor to investors and residents whose principle currency is something other than the Costa Rican colon. When you buy real estate with dollars in Costa Rica, it is immediately invested in a colón-denominated economy. Your dollar is converted into the colón until it is withdrawn back and converted back into dollars.

Inflation also figures substantially in the transaction, along with the rate of exchange. Once you make an investment in Costa Rica, your investment is subject to two independent inflation rates: The inflation rate of your country and that of Costa Rica.

The appreciation potential of any investment will be influenced by the factors mentioned above: devaluation of the colon, inflation in Costa Rica and inflation back home.

These factors won't affect you, however, if you want to simply live with colones and not convert them into dollars or if you buy and sell in areas like Escazú, where most transactions are done in dollars.

To fully understand dual-currency economics as well as all aspects of buying and selling property in Costa Rica, we highly recommend the book **"Rules of the Game"** by Bill Baker. For more information, write to 104 Half Moon Circle, H3, Hypoluxo, Florida 33462.

## *RENTAL PROPERTY*

The tenant is king in Costa Rica thanks to the archaic Lease Law (Ley de Inquilinato). A landlord cannot evict a tenant if the rent is paid on time unless the landlord can prove the property is needed for his/her personal use. Landlords can only raise the rent by a maximum of 15 percent per year. Unless otherwise specified in the contract, the lease will be valid for three years.

## SQUATTERS

Squatters can be a problem in Costa Rica, especially for the absentee property owner or for the buyer who rushes into a land purchase. Once a squatter has taken possession of the property, judicial intervention is required. Within the first three months from the time the squatter has taken possession, the procedure to oust is relatively simple. After the first three months, however, eviction can be complicated and time consuming. Regaining possession of a property that has been squatted for more than a year is still possible, but time consuming and costly. After 10 years the squatter can obtain legal right of the title. The moment you suspect a squatter has settled on your property, seek legal counsel.

## CURRENCY LAW

It is now possible to make contracts in dollars in Costa Rica. This has two positive effects. One, legal transactions in dollars give both buyer and seller a peace of mind previously unavailable. Investors needn't worry about devaluation of the colón, for example, or other difficulties caused by having to translate back and forth between dollars and colones.

And two, the possibility now exists of having mortgages in dollars. These mortgages are still seller-leveraged more often than not, but can be written by an attorney and guaranteed by the property. Once sellers understand the implications of being able to offer this type of mortgage, it will likely become the most common type of financing, spurred by the buyer's desire to keep property taxes lower. In Costa Rica a mortgage will automatically raise the declared value of the property to the amount of the mortgage.

## AT THE BEACH

"Judging by the soaring prices," one investor once noted. "Costa Rica's beaches aren't just fields of sand, but piles of tiny diamonds." However, real estate bargains can still be found in this country, depending on how hard you work to find them and how fast you move to buy. Beach property with access to infrastructure like running water, electricity, reasonable roads, and other services is going fast.

Most foreigners in Costa Rica settle in and around the capital of San José for improved access to shopping, health care, bilingual schools, finer restaurants and cultural life. With so many beautiful beaches some two-hours from home, however, it doesn't require much expense -- or excuse -- to head to the Pacific or Caribbean coast for a weekend of sun and sea. The following paragraphs detail some of the fastest growing beach areas. Many of these already enjoy a burgeoning foreign community.

**Flamingo/Tamarindo,** on the Pacific Northwest coast in the province of Guanacaste, has been attracting tourists and foreign residents for years. This is considered the country's "Gold Coast," because it is home to some of its most beautiful dry-tropical beaches and shorter rainy season.

The marina at Flamingo beach is the largest south of Acapulco, Mexico, and is popular with deep-sea anglers, who come for pleasure and competition.

Several half-million dollar homes gaze out over the white sands of Flamingo beach from high above, on the cliffs. Small beach condo's there sell from $150,000 to $300,000, and small finish lots from $40,000 to $200,000. This is considered Costa Rica's most expensive coastal area.

Heading south, you'll encounter the small beach towns of **Brasilito, Conchal and Grande**. Most foreigners settle in the larger communities of Flamingo, to the north, and Tamarindo, to the south, so good buys are still available in these beautiful and peaceful towns.

**Tamarindo** beach is considered the main population center on Costa Rica's "Gold Coast," with a large foreign population of hotel, restaurant and shop owners. Even so, the community remains decidedly "small town," with excellent beach access, tame surf and plenty of pelicans. Lots here sell from

$30,000 to $100,000 and beach condo's from $80,000 to $200,000.

About an hour-and-a-half south of Tamarindo lie the communities of **Nosara, Sámara** and **Carrillo**. The hillsides and forest are greener here due to slightly higher rainfall. Wildlife, such as iguanas, howler monkeys and parrots, are plentiful.

**Nosara** beach attracts many Swiss expat's, who operate small rental cabinas. **Carrillo** is a little harder to get to, but features a beautiful half-moon bay that is popular with swimmers, as well as the Guanamar hotel. Access to Carrillo, at the end of a bumpy road that sometimes floods-out during the rainy season, has kept many foreigners away, but offers much potential.

**Sámara** attracts tourists and residents of the neighboring communities with its nightlife, discos, restaurants. It's beach -- long, wide and breathtaking -- has been attracting visitors for years.

The **Jacó, Quepos** and **Manuel Antonio** beaches on the Central Pacific are all popular vacation and living spots, but for slightly different reasons.

At only an hour-and-a-half from San José, **Jacó** beach offers the city dweller the fastest and easiest access to sun and surf. It's a popular destination for both Ticos and foreigners wishing to escape the city for a day or weekend. The town of Jacó is well-developed with a healthy population of foreign shop and restaurant owners. Lush vegetation covers the hillsides and offers an amazing sight when viewed from the sea, but the brown sand and silty water from area rivers sends the more esthetic among us farther north or south in search of white sand and blue water.

**Quepos/Manuel Antonio** is considered by many to be the country's most beautiful beach. The site of a national park brimming with white-face monkeys, jungle rodents, iguanas, parrots, colorful amphibians and insects, this area has experienced a lot of growth over the last five years.

Nearly all of the area's small hotels, restaurants and cabinas are foreign-owned. As in Flamingo and Tamarindo, real estate in this area is among the country's most expensive, with small beach lots starting at $70,000. A condo here will set you back at least $80,000.

If you keep on "a-head'n" south along a wide gravel road, you'll finally bump and grind into **Dominical**. The superior surf at this beach has been attracting surfers for years, but its lower land prices have also been turning-heads lately. Beach lots here sell for around $40,000, while a five-acre farm with a small house could sell for as little as $60,000.

Amid the teeming rainforests of the southern **Osa Peninsula** springs the sleepy port town **Golfito**. In 1989, the government declared Golfito a "free port," where residents can buy electronics and household appliances without paying steep import taxes. The port revitalized what was once a dying banana town, and is now the center of activity and the region's biggest employer.

Thousands of Costa Ricans make a pilgrimage to Golfito once a year to stock-up or replace aging appliances. The entire town has dedicated itself to these pilgrims, offering a host of quality but inexpensive lodging and restaurants. The town doesn't offer much nightlife, but the locals want you, and your dollars, back, so they have become among the country's friendliest and most helpful.

Access to the peninsula is best by air or sea. Landslides and flooding frequently cut off road access during the rainy season. The area, one of the country's most beautiful and untouched, also offers among the best real estate values. Beach lots sell for around $30,000, and a five-acre farm with a small house goes for close to $50,000.

## *PACIFIC BEACH DEVELOPMENTS*

Guanacaste is home to some of the country's most innovative real estate development projects that spring from the area's unspoiled tropical forest and uncrowded beaches. Among the most successful are the following:

**Playa Hermosa**, near the Liberia international airport in the northern Pacific, is the site of Sol Playa Hermosa, one of the most successful beach development communities in the country. The project forms part of an existing facility with a proven track record, excellent financing, beautiful new villas and superior income potential. Only a few opportunities remain. For more information, call (506) 290-0506.

**Rancho Playa Negra** is a private seaside community located in a beautiful uncrowded area of Costa Rica's Gold Coast. The Rancho's more than 36 acres of gently rolling bluffs overlook the blue Pacific with spectacular views up and down the coast.

Ocean front lots average 1,500 square meters with a price of about $45,000. The lots vary in size down to 620 square meters, with some costing less than $10,000. The community has complete infrastructure including roads, electricity, water, 24-hour security, parks and community areas, and property management services. For more information call (506) 255-1001 or fax (506) 223-6048.

Located exactly in the middle of Costa Rica's two most famous and beautiful beaches, Conchal and Flamingo, **Kanes & Kanes** invites you to visit their newest project at Playa Brasilito, with one-and-a-half kilometers of frontage on the new Flamingo paved road and one kilometer of beach.

Five years ago, it would have been impossible to buy land fronting a paved road with all of the services and amenities that are available today, now being offered for as little as $10 per square meter.

The project features a golf course; marina; luxury hotel resort and pristine, white-sand beaches, where average land values run from $30 to $150 per square meter. K&K is offering only a limited number of one-hectare lots for just $10 per square meter. Financing is available at low interest rates.

For more information, call Tel: (506) 257-5352 or 257-5620, Fax: (506) 257-7385.

**Villas Euphoria** is an exclusive enclave of 45 large homesites distributed among forests and green zones on 17 hectares of rolling hills overlooking Carillo beach in the north Pacific. Each lot has spectacular views of the bay and coastline of the lush Nicoya Peninsula. The project has its own water system, private roads and a gated security entrance. It has easy access to a light-plane landing strip, marina and beach resorts of Carillo and Sámara. Lot sizes range from 1,000 to more than 5,000 square meters, with prices from $16,000 up to $100,000. For more information call (506) 255-1001 or Fax (506) 223-6048.

## *CARIBBEAN COAST*

The Atlantic Coast is still recovering from several murders and violent robberies committed a few years ago, as well as its reputation as a center for illegal drug activity.

Local merchants, hoteliers and longtime residents have organized and lobbied to make their community much safer and more tourist-friendly. Police are now friendly, casually dressed and plentiful. With its Caribbean flair, reggae music and native community feel, the Atlantic Coast not only offers some of the country's most beautiful beaches, but also a diversity of native culture that's hard to find elsewhere.

Real estate prices here are conservative, with Cahuita, Puerto Viejo, Punta Uva and Manzanillo the most sought-after sites. A two-and-a-half acre lot in this region sells for around $60,000.

## *REGULATIONS AT THE BEACH*

Costa Rica's coastline is all public. By law, the first 50 meters above the mean high tide line are inalienably public, defined by what is known as the '50-meter line.' No one can restrict access or have a totally private beach. There are some exceptions, but they include port areas, old land grants, and some titles prior to 1973.

**Maritime-Terrestrial Zone** On 80 to 85 percent of the coast, the 150 meters following the "50-meter line" is government-owned lease land, also known as the "maritime zone." Within this zone foreigners must establish five years' residency to own more than 49 percent of the rights to a lease.

Two loopholes include holding the lease with a corporation that is wholly owned by another corporation that is wholly owned by a foreigner, or by having a Costa Rican hold 51 percent of the lease in name only.

**Development of Maritime Zones** Development of the maritime zone does not discriminate against foreigners, but a regulating plan must exist. If one does not exist, the developer must create one and then have it approved by the Costa Rican Tourism Institute (ICE), the National Housing and Urbanization Institute (INVU) and the local municipality. Such a regulating plan will call for 'zoning' of the land, including public-use areas, roads, water, electricity, and more. This can be a time-consuming and expensive process, but it is absolutely necessary in order to develop lease land.

The other 15 to 20 percent of the coast is land that is 'titled' to the 50-meter line. That is to say that no maritime zone exists, and the landowner may develop without the inconvenience of filing a regulating plan. Tourism development must, of course, be approved by ICT, but almost anything else would require only building permits.

Naturally, with regard to prices, land titled to the 50-meter line is far more valuable and thus more expensive.

## BUILDING A HOME

**Buy or Build?** The decision between buying and building a home in Costa Rica is a big one. Most people thrill to the excitement and romance of moving to Costa Rica, but some are intimidated by the idea of building a home to suit their individual needs and desires.

Normally, a person who has made the decision to move here has a pretty good idea of what he or she wants to do, having given much thought to such a major change in lifestyle. In spite of this, many find the pickings slim with regard to existing homes. They like the idea of building a custom home, but are unsure of how best to go about it.

**Cost** The cost of building a typical home in Costa Rica depends on the quality of the finish, but prices range from $350 to $550 per square meter (10.76 square feet) of construction, not including land or such other amenities as a swimming pool. (Example: 1,000 square foot home would cost between $35,000 to $55,000.)

**Details** First, be sure to obtain a minimum option period of 30 days, so your architect can complete all pre-development studies, i.e. drainage, soils, zoning, utilities, etc. If all looks well, you and the architect will discuss preliminary design and budget and then proceed with the construction plans. A good architect will handle building permits; work with your contractor and oversee the construction.

Second, get written quotes for the construction from at least three contractors. Make sure the quotes include everything: construction, engineering and inspection fees (these are all determined by the Architects and Engineers Association). If your contractor can provide all these services, the project will be completed much more efficiently. After you choose your contractor, always obtain independent legal counsel. The contractor will draw up an agreement outlining all costs, services, and responsibilities. Have your attorney review this and approve it before you sign.

**Plan Approvals** Architecture and engineering are completed in this next phase. This normally takes about six weeks, but will vary according to each project. After approval of the final design, the plans will be submitted for approvals to the Association of Architects and Engineers, the municipality and, for tourist-oriented developments, to ICT. These approvals take about six weeks.

**Time Frame** The following is a typical time schedule to design, obtain permits and construct of a 1,000 square-foot home:

| | | |
|---|---|---|
| 1. Preliminary studies, design: | | 6 weeks |
| 2. Construction plans: | | 6 weeks |
| 3. Building permits: | | 8 weeks |
| 4. Construction: | | <u>32 weeks</u> |
| | **Total:** | 52 weeks |

**Shortcuts** The use of prefabricated materials will shorten the permitting and construction phases of the project. There are several companies in Costa Rica that make high-quality products that help minimize expensive and time-consuming on-site work. Costs are competitive and risks are low. If this option appeals to you, or you would like more information before deciding, mention it to your architect, engineer and builder as early in the process as you can.

**Personal Site Visits** Once construction begins, visit the site frequently and keep an eagle eye on the workers. This will give you a better idea of the time involved, the quality of the work, and any possible changes in materials or design that you may want to make.

If you cannot inspect the site, have someone you trust do it for you. Insist that your contractor submit written progress reports to you with requests for payments that correspond with your construction schedule. Operating lines of credit are expensive here; it is more typical to pay partials in advance for work to be completed.

**Municipal Site Inspections** Municipalities here are not responsible for construction inspections, so make sure you obtain a signed inspection report from the responsible engineers, as they are legally responsible for completion according to plans. It is common to hold 5 to 10 percent of the construction funds back for 15 to 30 days after completion to ensure that the contractor will correct any errors or deficiencies that may come up after you move in.

**Bonding** Bonding of construction companies is not typical in Costa Rica. Always choose a contractor with a proven record.

We've found that the San José Architect Firm Carlos Ossenbach and Asociados, Tel: (506) 253-6596, is capable of handling all aspects of design and construction management from houses to large hotels and commercial projects. The firm Roman Hernández and Assoc. is also popular with expat's seeking professional service for projects of all sizes. Call them at (506) 381-9482.

## Tips for Success

*The two biggest mistakes made by foreigners who buy real estate in Costa Rica is not properly researching the title for hidden liens and not considering the access to water and electricity. These measures are easy to confirm through the National Registry and local municipality -- don't ever take the word of the seller; investigate the property yourself!*

### Metric System Land Conversion

1 mile=1.61 kilometers
1 kilometer=0.62 miles
1 meter=3.28 feet
1 yard=0.914 meters
1 sq. meter=10.76 sq. feet
1 sq. foot=0.093 sq. meters
1 acre=43,560 sq. feet
1 hectare=10,000 sq. meters
1 inch=2.54 centimeters
1 acre=0.405 hectares
1 manzana=1.73 acres
1 hectare=2.47 acres
1 manzana=6,989 sq. meters

# HEALTH OPTIONS

Modern, first-rate, and affordable medical and dental procedures are available in Costa Rica, where the socialized medical system ranks up near the U.S. and Canada as one of the best in the world.

A 1992 study at the University of Costa Rica determined that 6 percent of tourists visit doctors while here. Most choose this destination for excellent cosmetic surgery and others make the trip for dental work or heart surgery. Many health tourists combine recovery and healing time with trips to Costa Rica's beautiful tropical beaches or incomparable rain forest parks and reserves.

## *TROPICAL DISEASES*

Costa Rica is a regional leader in the prevention of tropical diseases, but has not been immune to them. Travelers here may often be exposed to the potentially deadly threats of dengue, malaria and cholera. The following is a brief explanation of the causes, symptoms and treatment of each:

**Dengue** Costa Rica is home to three strains of dengue, which is transmitted by Aedes aegypti, a small mosquito with distinctive white stripes on its legs. Symptoms include headaches, high fever (39 to 40 C.), pain in the muscles and joints and behind the eyes and, in some cases, diarrhea and vomiting.

A second infection by a different strain of the disease could cause the deadly hemorrhagic dengue. Victims of this strain may experience dots of blood on the skin, nasal or gum bleeding, or irregular vaginal bleeding. The worse cases go into "dengue shock," which is distinguished by low temperature, clammy skin, paleness, stomach pain, loss of consciousness and rapid, weak pulse.

The best prevention for all mosquito-carried diseases is to eliminate pools of fresh water in old tires, flower pots etc. that serve as breeding grounds. Insect repellent, light weight protective clothing and the use of a mosquito net for sleeping also reduce the risk, as well as spraying a household insecticide underneath beds and other low, dark places.

**Malaria** Costa Rica has yet to experience a fatal strain of malaria, but this red-blood-cell-attacking disease has hit the Atlantic Coast especially hard.

Symptoms are similar to those of regular dengue. Travelers visiting the Atlantic port city of Limón or the northern regions of San Carlos, Los Chiles and Sarapiquí should use insect repellent after sundown, use a mosquito net for sleeping and take precautions similar to those for dengue. The risk for this disease is higher during the rainy season, from May to November.

Visitors are also urged to take two tablets (300 mg.) of chloroquine (trade name Aralen) once a week, two weeks before arriving and six weeks after leaving.

If you suspect you have malaria, report to the nearest medical facility immediately. Do not self-medicate.

**Cholera** The few cases of cholera have been reported in Costa Rica have largely been attributed to people who contracted the disease while in a neighboring country.

Victims of the vibrio cholerae bacteria, caused by impurities in food and water, suffer explosive, watery diarrhea, vomiting, clammy skin and muscle pain.

Dehydration is the victim's greatest threat, and should be combatted with massive intake of oral rehydration solution (*suero oral*), sold in pharmacies. Rehydration solution can also be made by mixing two level tablespoons of sugar or honey and one-half teaspoon of salt in one liter of water. The sufferer should also continue eating foods such as cereals, bananas, citric fruit juices, yogurt, cheese and eggs.

Extreme cleanliness will prevent the disease. If you suspect cholera is a threat, boil water for drinking, brushing teeth or making ice. Peel all fruit before eating. Thoroughly clean all vegetables by soaking them in water with lemon juice, and avoid eating seafood. Generally, these extremes are unnecessary in Costa Rica.

## COSTA RICA'S MEDICAL SYSTEM

Although the nation's Social Security System provides practically every citizen with guaranteed health care, many private practices and clinics function as higher-priced alternatives to the long lines and bureaucracy of socialized medicine. These facilities, often staffed by doctors trained abroad, have become popular with tourists and residents because of the comparatively low-priced procedures available.

### VITAL STATISTICS

| | |
|---|---|
| Life expectancy | 76 years |
| Infant mortality per 1,000 live births | 14 |
| Average number of children per woman | 3.2 |
| % of minimum daily calories received | 121% |
| Percent of fully immunized 1-year-olds | 93% |
| Physicians per 10,000 people | 12.5 |
| Access to safe water | 94% |
| Access to health, sewage and sanitation | 97% |
| Public health expenditure as % of GDP | 3% |

*Source: Inside Costa Rica, by Silvia Lara, Tom Barry and Peter Simonson*

**Top Quality** The attractive costs do not reflect a lack of quality, which is every bit what it is in the so-called First World, but rather the country's cheaper overhead costs, lab fees and malpractice insurance. Over the last 20 years, health tourism has boomed here, to the point that foreigners occupy, at times, up to a fifth of the beds in these clinics.

The **Clínica Bíblica**, located in downtown San José, and the **Clínica Católica**, in the north San José district of Guadalupe, provide complete hospital and emergency services. The U.S.-trained doctors at the **Clínica Americana**, also downtown, offer outpatient service and are on-call 24-hours a day. The staff at the **KOP Medical Clinic** in the west San José suburb of Escazú, speaks English, French, and Spanish. Their range of services includes gynecology and obstetrics, dermatology, psychology, and pediatrics.

Call the Clínica Bíblica at (506) 257-5252, the Clínica Católica at (506)225-5055, the Clínica Americana at (506) 222-1010 and the KOP Medical Clinic at (506) 228-4119.

**Low Cost** Office visits at most clinics and hospitals cost between $20.00 and $30.00, though it can be more if the doctor is a specialist. Although prescription drugs are imported, and may end up being the largest cost if you have an emergency room visit, they still cost considerably less than in the U.S. Laboratory tests and analysis are also significantly cheaper.

**Health Tourism** Thus far, health tourism in Costa Rica is mostly promoted by word-of-mouth and personal references from satisfied clients. The Costa Rican Tourism Institute (ICT) has no health tourism promotional campaign, mostly because professional doctors' societies here, including the Society of Plastic Surgeons, consider it unethical for doctors to advertise or reveal the cost of their services.

In recent years, however, plastic surgeons and cosmetic dentists have begun to circulate informational and price pamphlets abroad, and even to cite prices for articles in foreign magazines.

## GENERAL PHYSICIAN

Dr. Bruce Gale is a pediatrician and general physician. He has lived in Costa Rica for more than 30 years, but is originally from Wheaton, Illinois. Dr. Gale studied at the University of Illinois, Minnesota and Costa Rica. He has many years experience.

After 21 years practicing medicine at San José's Clínica Bíblica, he relocated to the Centro Médico San Vicente in Heredia, just 25 minutes northwest of the capital.

The cost for an office visit is $22.00. Dr. Gale is located 125 meters east of the Heredia Hospital. Office phone: (506) 260-2211; home: (506) 260-1079; emergencies: (506) 225-2500; Fax: (506) 237-1980. He can also be reached by mail at Apdo. 1738-3000, Heredia, Costa Rica.

## PLASTIC SURGERY

People from all over the world come to Costa Rica for cosmetic and reconstructive surgery from pleasant, highly professional doctors, and at prices that are substantially lower than in the U.S. and Europe.

Plastic surgeons here use the latest equipment, including lasers, and keep up on trends, regularly attending professional conferences and meetings here and abroad.

A patient planning on surgery in Costa Rica must provide the doctor with a medical history; undergo a complete check up, including electrocardiogram,; complete blood and urine tests and receive an HIV test. The latter may need to be repeated in Costa Rica before surgery. Front and side facial photo views are recommended for those coming for facial surgery.

Many doctors ask that people not smoke or drink alcohol two weeks before and several weeks after surgery, to hasten healing. They also say it's important to lose weight before plastic surgery, not after, because skin will hang loose if you lose weight post-procedure. Most said they don't do liposuction of fat deposits on overweight people, but only on people who have lost a lot of weight and who still have unsightly deposits.

Some of the most popular procedures and estimated, average prices are as follows:

**Full Face Lift** The most popular plastic surgery is still a full face lift, or rhytidectomy. A patient can expect to pay about $700 for a two-day hospital stay after the procedure, allowing two weeks for full recuperation. The doctor's services will range between $2,000 and $3,500. These full face lifts are more complete than the average North American face lift, and include forehead, eyes, injections of fat, and even a touch to the nose. Doctors do not recommend a first face lift before the age of 45 or 50. The following list should give you an idea about the approximate rates for common procedures:

- Rhinoplasty, or nose surgery, $1,600 to $2,500.

- Breast reduction, $1,900 to $3,000.

- Abdominal liposuction and tummy tuck, $1,900 to $3,000. This includes muscle surgery and tightening of the skin. All doctors here agree this is not an operation for overweight people, and only indicated when a scar is preferable to a defect, such as hanging skin.

- Liposuction, $800 to $1,500.

- Blepharoplast, or eyelid surgery, costs $200 for the hospital, and the doctor's fee is between $750 and $2,200.

- Complete breast reconstruction (following a mastectomy) can cost $4,000.

Doctors here also do dermabrasion, reconstruction of scars, and collagen or other treatment to augment lips. Best known doctors and clinics are as follows:

**Dr. Arnoldo Fournier,** a founding member of Costa Rica's Plastic Surgery and one of the country's biggest names in the business, works out of Santa Rita Clinic. He studied plastic reconstructive surgery in Mexico and in Saint Luke's Hospital Columbia University, New York. His foreign patients have increased from one or two every month, to two a week.

Dr. Fournier is one of the few surgeons here who advertises aggressively, and he offers several package plans which include rooms, at a little less than the normal rate, at the four star San José Palacio Hotel. A face lift, abdominal liposuction and tummy tuck, or breast reduction package includes: three days in the hospital for $800, 12 days in the hotel for $1,200, and $2,500-$4,000 in surgery and doctor's fees.

A breast implant package includes surgery and doctor's fees of $2,500 to $3,500, two-day hospital stay for $800 and ten days at the hotel for $1,000. For a free brochure and information, please contact: Mrs. Madeleine Arango, Office Manager, 10420 SW. Court, Miami, Florida 33176, Tel/Fax (305) 271-9297. Phone 222-1010, fax 255-4370, address Apdo. 117-1002, San José.

**Rodrigo Araya, M.D.** is a member of Costa Rica's Plastic Surgeons Society. He has studied plastic and reconstructive surgery at the University of Mexico and is also a U.S. trained Plastic Surgeon. He operates in the Clínica Santa Rita and the Clínica Bíblica and is part of the reconstructive surgery team at the San Juan de Dios Hospital.

He says most of his patients come from the U.S. and Canada. He lodges his patients in his "house of recovery" at an average cost of $60.00 per day. This includes meals and all postoperative medical care. One family member may join the patient in this house for an additional $60.00, if notified ahead of time. Also included is the transportation from the airport to his clinic and all visits to the doctor. English spoken. Tel: (506) 297-2060, 297-0907; Tel/Fax: (506) 283-4296; beeper: (506) 233-3333. Address: PO Box 12088-1000, San José, Costa Rica.

**Dr. Gabriela Guzmán-Stein** is a candidate member of the American Board of Plastic Surgeons. She graduated from the University of Guadalajara, Mexico in 1981 and underwent eight years of general surgery at the University of Minnesota Hospital.

While in Minnesota, she did a research fellowship in plastic surgery and completed her research fellowship in microsurgery at Case Western Hospital.

She received her plastic surgery training at the University of Alabama, Birmingham and was then sent to Australia to complete a fellowship in craniofacial surgery. She later returned as an assistant professor to the University of Alabama, where she remained until July 1994.

Dr. Guzmán-Stein is the author of several publications in accredited journals and several book chapters. She is internationally known and respected for the development of new techniques. She resides in Costa Rica, where she was born, but is licensed to practice in four U.S. states. She is a diplomat of the American Board of Surgeons.

Dr. Guzmán-Stein's clinic provides the following services: Liposculpture, old liposuction, breast enlargement, reduction, lift or reconstruction, eyelid surgery, facelift, forehead lift, nose surgery, tummy tuck, chin or cheek implants, ear surgery, scar revisions, dermabrasions, scalp baldness surgery, hair transplant, thigh lift. She also offers endoscopic surgery.

For more information contact her office in Costa Rica, Tel: (506) 221-3241, Home (506) 487-7527 (weekends only), or write to PO Box 1519-1000, San Jose, Costa Rica. In the U.S., contact her Miami office and ask for Inés van der Ree, Tel: (305) 261-1667, home (305) 597-0376, Fax: (305) 261-3521.

**Dr. Ernesto Martén,** member of the American Board of Plastic Surgery, says a high percentage of his clients are foreigners. He has his own clinic where he operates and where patients stay until totally recovered. Phone (506) 224-4738, address Clínica Martén, Apdo. 889-1000 San José.

**Dr. Luis Antonio Murillo Cordero**, practiced two years as a plastic surgeon in Brazil and estimates that 40 percent of his clients come from outside the country. He operates in the Clínica Santa Rita and the Clínica Bíblica. Phone (506) 233-5656, address Centro Médico Metropolitano, Ave. 4, Calles 22-24, San José.

## *HEART SURGERY*

More and more U.S. patients are coming to Clínica Bíblica (257-5252) for heart bypass surgery, according to Dr. Juan Bautista Pérez, medical director of the hospital. Most clients come on personal reference, and prospective patients must provide satisfactory studies, done in the home country.

Dr. Manuel Sánez Madrigal, associate fellow of the American College of Cardiology and member of the hospital's heart team, says a bypass can cost $15,000-$18,000 -- one third of what it costs in the States.

The price includes surgery, anesthesiology, hospitalization, intensive care, doctors and nurses. Most patients stay in the hospital six to eight days and then remain in the country a few weeks for follow-up and monitoring.

The Clínica Bíblica Hospital has been serving the Costa Rican people since 1929. This hospital has a team of English-speaking doctors, including surgeons that have been trained in the University of Costa Rica, Mexico, Argentina, London and the United States.

The Clínica Bíblica is equipped to handle practically any emergency on a 24-hour basis. Services include: a drugstore open 24 hours a day, laboratory, full hospitalization service, ambulance service, diabetic clinic, magnetic resonance imaging (MRI) and computed tomography (CT). Specialties to be found at the hospital include: family practice, gynecology obstetrics, internal medicine, ophthalmology, orthopedics, otorhino-laryngology, pediatrics and geriatrics.

Clínica Bíblica is located on Ave. 14, Calle Central and 1. Hospital phone (506) 257-5252, Fax (506) 255-4947;

emergency phone (506) 257-0466, Fax: (506) 223-7676; mailing address P.O. Box 1307, San José, Costa Rica.

## DENTAL CARE AND COSMETIC DENTISTRY

Many dentists in Costa Rica speak English and also offer excellent dental care and cosmetic procedures at prices about one-third lower than in the U.S.

Some popular procedures for foreigners, and average price estimates, include the following. Most doctors charge an additional $35 for an initial examination, as well as extra for any necessary X-rays.

- Root form osseous-integrated implants: $750
  Prosthetic reconstruction varies with the type of restoration needed, but is usually 30 to 50 percent less than in the U.S., with the same quality materials and professionals who are up-to-date on procedures.
- Porcelain laminates, per tooth, $130.
- Fillings for cavity, per tooth, $20.
- Inlay or onlay, per tooth: semi-precious $150, yellow gold $190, porcelain $145, chrome $95.
- Single root canal, $110.
- Removable chrome nickel bridge, $250.
- Rigid metal-porcelain bridge, $180-$210.
- Complete prosthesis, $200.
- Wisdom tooth surgery, $150.
- Tooth extraction, $30.

**Dr. Bernal Pacheco Rawson** has a new and modern clinic in San José. He graduated from the University of Missouri, Kansas City, and is a prosthodontics specialist in bridges and implants. Phone his office at (506) 223-7905, Fax: (506) 227-4735. Emergency beeper: 233-3333. Home: 441-3992.

**Dr. Estaban Bolaños Lund, DDS, MScD** is a registered specialist in periodontics that limits his practice to periodontics and dental osseointegrated implants. He graduated from the Dental School and Hospital, University Hospital of Wales, UK, and is an international member of both the American Academy of Periodontology and the Academy of Osseointegration, as well as a diplomat from the American society of Osseointegration. He is also president of the Costa Rican Academy of Periodontology.

Dr. Bolaños treats his patients out of his own periodontal clinic in the north San José district of Guadalupe, and also at the La Rambla shopping center in Escazú. He has been involved in periodontics since 1978 and in dental osseointegrated implants since 1988.

For more information, call his periodontal clinic at (506) 297-1898; fax, (506) 236-1884; address, PO box 114-6151, Santa Ana 2000, Costa Rica; e-mail: <ebolanos@sol.racsa.co.cr>

**Dr. Luis Kaver Fastag** heads a modern clinic for cosmetic and restorative dentistry that specializes in porcelain crowns, implants, porcelain laminates, inlays and onlays, gold precision bridges and bleaching. His clinic uses an intra oral video camera with computer, so the patient can see his or her teeth before and after the dental work is completed.

Dr. Kaver is a graduate in cosmetic dentistry from Baylor College of Dentistry, Dallas, Texas. His clinic is run according to the American Dental Association regulations on hygiene and sterilization and is a member of the American Academy of Cosmetic Dentistry.

Dr. Kaver invites you to stop by and visit his clinic, located 100 meters south of the Sabana McDonald's, or give him a call at (506) 290-2323, Fax: (506) 290-0303. Mailing address: Apdo. 292-1007, San José.

**Dr. Ronald H. De Pass Jiménez** recently expanded his Specialty Dental Center. The center specializes in porcelain crowns and bridges, implants, porcelain laminates, inlays and onlays, gold crowns, full mouth prosthesis, removable semi-precision bridges, nitrous oxide sedation for apprehensive patients, root canal, facial surgery, panoramic radiographs, gum surgery and maxillo.

The clinic is run according to the American Dental Association regulations on hygiene and sterilization and are members of the American Dental Association. The new center is located in Sabana Sur, 100 meters east and 75 meters south of McDonald's. Tel (506) 296-1700, Fax (506) 231-2990.

**Dr. Mario E. Garita** is a well-known specialist in implant dentistry. He lectures in Costa Rica and all over North and South America. His grandfather and father taught hospital dentistry, and his wife is a general dentist.

Dr. Garita has trained many doctors in both surgical and prosthetic areas of implantology. He trained at the university of Miami School of Medicine, where he lived for two years while acquiring his degree.

Dr. Garita handles most of Costa Rica's difficult implant cases due to his extensive training in osseous reconstruction. He is also the director of The Center for Dental Implants of Costa Rica, a specially designed office for treating implant patients. A certified anesthesiologist handles the I.V. sedation and general anesthesia cases. They also provide prosthodontist, general dentistry and endodontist services in the same office. This center uses only American Dental Association (ADA) certified implant systems, which boast a 95 to 98 percent success rate. For more information call or Fax (506) 290-1750, or write to PO Box 333-1200, San José, Costa Rica. USA address: Interlink 320, PO box 02-5635, Miami, FL, 33102.

 **Tips for Success**

*Quality, low-cost health care is the most important benefit of life in Costa Rica. While most foreign residents feel comfortable "going under the knife" here for surgeries such as gall stones or appendectomies, for delicate or unusual surgical procedures many prefer to travel to the U.S.*

# MEDICAL INSURANCE

Insurance in Costa Rica is handled exclusively by the National Insurance Institute (INS), a state monopoly established in 1924. Because it sells such high volumes, it is rated among the largest insurance companies in Latin America.

For years, the government has considered opening up the insurance market to private providers and may actually do it in the coming years. In the meantime, however, clients may choose any company they wish... as long as it's the INS!

To qualify for insurance while living or traveling in Costa Rica, your legal status is not important. Everyone is eligible to apply. All foreign applicants are required to undergo a urine test. Applicants older than 60 must also submit an electrocardiogram, while those over 70 must be examined by an INS doctor. The INS will not insure anyone older than 100.

### 1997 Annual Insurance Policy Costs

| Age | Male | Age | Female |
|---|---|---|---|
| 18-39 | $325 | 18-36 | $670 |
| 40-49 | $485 | 37-46 | $560 |
| 50-59 | $510 | 47-56 | $510 |
| 60-70 | $600 | 57-70 | $600 |

**Group policies enjoy an approximate 20 percent discount over individual rates**

For up-to-date information on Costa Rican insurance and friendly assistance in English when applying for a policy, we at OG books highly recommend Garrett and Associates. The Garrett brothers, Mike and Dave, are longtime residents of Costa Rica who have been helping newcomers painlessly wade through the red tape for years. Give them a call at (506) 233-2455.

The policy will cover your medical expenses in foreign countries, where you must pay for the services yourself and then submit a claim for reimbursement. The INS will pay according to actual costs in Costa Rica. Example: If you undergo surgery in the United States that costs $3,000, but the same treatment costs $2,000 in Costa Rica, you will only be reimbursed $2,000. This system is not very practical, however, because of the double deductible, as well as excessive bureaucratic red tape on the part of INS.

When you buy a policy, INS supplies you with an identification card and booklet that lists some 350 names of "affiliated" providers, such as hospitals, doctors, labs and pharmacies. When you use any of the listed providers, you pay only the deductible, which is 20 percent for labs, X-rays, cardiograms, medicines, treatments, etc., and 30 percent for ultrasound. All surgeries are covered 100 percent.

If you go to a "non-affiliated" organization, you must pay at time of service and then submit a claim to INS for reimbursement. INS will reimburse only up to the amount listed on its price schedule. Reimbursement takes some six weeks. As always, your agent will assist you in these procedures.

At present, medical policies have a ceiling of about $22,500 per person per year. This corresponds to an allocation of 10 percent for outpatient services and 90 percent for complete hospitalization.

Now, if you are asking yourself whether a $22,500 coverage a year will be adequate, the answer is a resounding "yes." Costa Rica's medical costs are much lower than in the United States and other developed countries -- and the service is top rate. So, don't worry! It's enough.

In fact, many Costa Ricans who live in the United States, as well as U.S. citizens, travel to Costa Rica exclusively for its medical and dental care. The savings frequently cover travel expenses and even entertainment while in-country!

### Tips for Success

*Most expatriates maintain their insurance coverage back home, but switch to a higher deductible. This gives them the option of returning to the U.S. for delicate surgeries or treatment of serious conditions.*

*Most U.S. insurance policies don't cover health expenses incurred abroad. Be sure you check with your agent before you move. The following list will help put you in touch with international insurance providers:*

| | |
|---|---|
| Travel Med | 1-800-732-5309 or (301) 296-5225 |
| Health Care Abroad | 1-800-237-6615 or (703) 281-9500 |
| Travel Assistance Int'l | 1-800-821-2828 or (202) 331-1609 |
| Access America | 1-800-284-8300 or (212) 490-5345 |
| World Care Travel Assist. | 1-800-253-1877 or (213) 749-1358 |
| Care Free Travel Insurance | 1-800-645-2424 or (516) 294-0220 |
| International SOS | 1-800-523-8930 or (215) 244-1500 |

*Ask your provider about emergency evacuation service to a U.S. hospital for urgent or delicate medical attention. Some companies provide air-ambulance service with on-board doctors and nurses, trip coordinators and global communications capabilities. Many also arrange stretcher transportation on commercial airlines. A few of these providers are:*

| | |
|---|---|
| National Jets | 1-800-327-3710 |
| North American Air Ambulance | 1-800-322-8167 |
| International SOS | 1-800-523-8930 |
| Air Ambulance Network | 1-800-387-1966 |
| Air Ambulance Int'l | 1-800-227-9996 |
| Life Flight | 1-800-231-4357 |

A $20,000 Costa Rican home.

Costa Rica is famous for its pretty women, called "Ticas."

Only five minutes from bustling San José, the quiet life of the countryside, with its old campesino homes, can still be appreciated.

Costa Rica offers modern, first-rate dental care and cosmetic procedures.

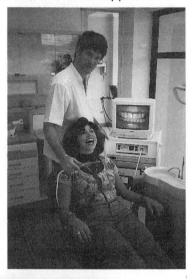

Recently released U.S. films are shown in English with Spanish sub-titles, at a cost of about $2.50.

High walls that surround many private residences offer privacy and security.

For about $2.50, you can buy a complete meal in a soda restaurant.

The exclusive Costa Rica Country Club has a 9-hole golf course, nine tennis courts, swimming pool and gym facilities.

Do you know the way to San José....

Four large, modern shopping malls offer variety and security, and are popular for meeting, having lunch and socializing.

At Saturday morning farmers markets, a couple can buy enough fresh fruits and vegetables to last a week for about $7.00.

Five Tica sisters wait for the bus to take them to Sunday mass.

No neighborhood or "barrio" is without at least one corner grocery store, called a "pulpería."

1,200 sq. ft. construction, 3-bedroom, 2-bath, maid's quarters, 20,000 sq. ft. lot: Sale Price, $60,000.

Many foreigners buy large homes and convert them into bed and breakfasts.

All public schools in Costa Rica require their students to wear uniforms that bear each learning center's unique, embroidered insignia.

A private mail service such as Star Box offers a more efficient alternative to the Costa Rican national postal service.

Aerial view of Sol Playa Hermosa, a popular beach living community.

Several big name resorts offer deluxe accommodations among the unspoiled tropical forests and pristine beaches.

Beautiful, unspoiled and un-crowded beaches line the Pacific and Caribbean coasts.

Trendy leisure time activities like pool can become lucrative business opportunities for foreigners.

A Costa Rican family takes a Saturday morning spin on their trusty Vespa motor scooter.

Street vendors like José will deliver fresh fruits and vegetables to your door step.

Small rental cabins or "cabinas" are a popular and often lucrative investment that requires considerable start-up capital.

Live-in housekeepers earn around $150 per month.

U.S. franchises can offer excellent money-making opportunities.

Businesses, such as this fresh orange juice stand, have low start-up expense and capitalize on the constant availability of a local product.

Importing fine Cuban cigars is another low start-up business that really pulls in the profits.

Many guide books are already offered on the local market, but room still exists for innovative and creative publishers with a lot of energy.

# MAKING MONEY

First-time visitors to Costa Rica often find that the nation's colorful blue and red currency makes investing here seem like playing monopoly.

Longtime residents often nod sagely when they hear this, but they know that the money is real enough!

The business climate in Costa Rica is stable and can be very profitable, but if you don't test the waters and do your homework, your experience can be just as disastrous as landing your token on St. Charles Place, complete with hotel.

Business conditions should keep improving. Successive governments have been moving away from state controls and towards an open economy in anticipation of free trade pacts with the United States, Mexico, Chile, Venezuela and Colombia.

Controls on the exchange of foreign currency have been eliminated. Private banks now can compete on an equal footing with state-owned banks. Foreigners are allowed to own their land outright.

The telecommunications system is as good as anything you'll find in a developing country, and officials are working on eliminating its current shortage of telephone lines. The information highway is easily accessed on various networks at reasonable prices.

Electricity is generated from both petroleum and hydroelectric sources, thus ensuring a hedge against shortage. The current infrastructure generally is able to satisfy demands.

Potable water is available in most of the Central Valley. Sanitation habits are high. While Guatemala faces 1,000 cases cholera per week, Costa Rica has reported only a handful of cases and each is rapidly attended.

Politically speaking, the country is undoubtedly the most stable in the region.

One reason for the stability is many of the social benefits offered, such as a good education system, free cradle-to-grave health care system and other rewards, such as the "aguinaldo" — a legally-mandated paycheck equivalent to a month's salary that every employer must give every employee each December.

Anyone who plans on becoming a future employer must realize that they are responsible for paying these costs. Whereas a worker might receive a $2.00 an hour salary, Constitutionally guaranteed social obligations can push up the real salary another 50 percent.

Governments have granted many rights throughout the years to workers -- that might be irksome for foreign business owners, but it's part of the hard-earned peace won by Costa Ricans.

Investors should also be aware of how the government, just like in the United States, can change its rulebook.

Due to pressure from international lending institutions, the government has taken various tax incentives away from areas such as tourism, reforestation and retirees.

Remember that despite appearances of similarity, the rules can be very different from those of the United States, so don't rush into investments and beware of fraud.

Talk to many locals and listen to what they tell you. They'll have heard of swindles and shady characters that have been preying on the innocence of the newcomer for years. If they tell you to be leery of a particular deal, you'd better listen!

Be wary of foreigners who seem to know their way around and try to impress you with their fluency in Spanish -- fluency helps, but is no substitute for honesty and integrity.

## WHO ARE THE CONSUMERS?

Slightly more than half of Costa Rica's 3.5 million inhabitants live in and around the capital city of San José. At only 3.66 square miles (9.47 sq. km.), San José is the hub of the country's political, economic, cultural and bureaucratic activity and the focal point of some 12 surrounding bedroom and commerce communities that form the greater San José metropolitan area.

Forty four percent of the population is under 20, 33 percent is aged 20 to 39, 15.6 percent from 40 to 59 and 7 percent is aged 60 or older.

Costa Rica is an educated country, with a 93 percent literacy rate, but this figure generally drops in very rural areas. The last population and vital statistic census was done in 1984, making accurate information hard to come by. Currently about 25 percent of the country's total population of 3 million is enrolled in elementary school, 9 percent is enrolled in secondary school and 8 percent in the country's universities.

Accurate statistics on socioeconomic levels lumps the population into two categories: poor and not poor. Breakdowns for the size of the country's upper, middle and lower classes haven't been updated since the 1984 census, but the vast majority of Ticos earn less than $500 per month.

**Upper Class** The leading salary earner in an upper-class Costa Rican household tends to be a top executive, company owner or non-managerial professional, such as lawyer or doctor. They tend to shop for groceries at supermarkets and specialty shops and buy clothing and durable goods in department stores, boutiques or in the U.S. Typical salary: More than $2,000 per month.

**Middle Class** The middle class salary earner tends to be an employed professional, civil servant, entrepreneur or small business person. This group usually shops for groceries at supermarkets, convenience stores, wholesale markets and some speciality stores. For clothing and durable goods, this group frequents department stores and, to a lesser extent, boutiques, or heads to the U.S. or Panama for better bargains, budget permitting. Many turn to neighborhood tailors or seamstresses to have their clothing made. This is usually a more economical option than store-bought clothing. Typical salary: $500 to $1,500.

**Lower Class** Lower class wage earners usually work in blue collar jobs, such as store clerk, mechanic, office assistant, secretary or security guard. They buy produce at farmers markets and groceries at wholesale markets or supermarkets. They have their clothing made locally or purchase in discount stores, market stalls or from street vendors. Typical salary: $100 to $500.

The country's largest cities and population centers are usually the "capitals" of the seven provinces, San José, Alajuela, Heredia, Cartago, Puntarenas, Liberia (Guanacaste) and Limón. Other principal towns include the southern community of San Isidro de El General, the northern town of Ciudad Quesada and the peninsular community of Nicoya.

Fully one-third of the country's total population lives in San José and its many surrounding districts.

## *THE OVERSEAS ENTREPRENEUR*

Even inexperienced entrepreneurs feel they are in their element when going abroad to start a business. Language barriers and cultural clashes become easier to overcome once they see the broader picture of limitless opportunities, low start-up costs and few competitors. More and more entrepreneurs are confronting these challenges abroad in anticipation of the payoff ahead.

In Costa Rica, the hard working individual can start from scratch without burdensome regulations and high taxes faced by businesses back home. The emerging entrepreneur's ideas and actions go beyond personal profits; they will help shape the country now and into the future. Many of the same businesses that have already succeeded in the U.S. and Canada will also succeed in Costa Rica — the door of opportunity opens widest to those who can adapt tried and true concepts to the Central American market.

U.S.-style goods and services are more sought-after here than anywhere else in the world. As you travel in Costa Rica, you will notice a need for many of the products and services that everyone back home takes for granted. That old submarine sandwich shop you'd been frequenting since you were a kid, or the dry cleaners right around the corner, are often franchises that could be even more lucrative south-of-the-border. By providing a more efficient, better quality service than already exists, you even have a shot at shaking the foundations of long-established, but mediocre local businesses.

Cemaco, for instance, is now the leading department store in Costa Rica. Its founders opened their first store here because when they were constructing their home, they discovered they had to go to Miami to buy the quality furnishings and fixtures they were looking for. Ten years later, they now have five stores and a lot of enthusiastic and loyal customers.

You might even discover an idea or service never seen before. Two young Canadian men recently constructed a series of small platforms among the tropical rainforest treetops and now offer "Canopy Tours" to adventurous tourists, who, suspended by ropes and cables, swing from platform to platform getting to know nature up-close and personal. Their innovative idea has been the subject of many local news stories, as they continue to scale, roll and swing toward success.

## *WHY COSTA RICA?*

So, of all the places you could go to experiment with your entrepreneurial prowess, why choose Costa Rica? The reasons are as numerous as the opportunities, but here are just a few:

## Rights to Private Ownership and Establishment

The country offers many options for business start-up. Except for the very few endeavors expressly reserved for the State, such as telecommunications or electricity generation, all entities and persons, may establish and own businesses and engage in remunerative activity.

Even in the sectors traditionally limited to State control, the trend over the last few years has definitely been toward privatization and improved competition. One of the country's hottest public debates regards the future of its giant telecommunications and electricity company, ICE, which enjoys a Constitutionally guaranteed national monopoly. Even

### WHY VISITORS COME TO COSTA RICA

| Activity | % who do it |
|---|---|
| Sun and beach | 62.2 |
| Sport fishing | 6.8 |
| Surfing | 7.4 |
| Diving/snorkeling | 17.5 |
| Rafting/kayaking | 11.7 |
| Other sports activities | 5.2 |
| Natural history | 45.6 |
| Birdwatching | 32.3 |
| Visit family/friends | 17.7 |
| Seminars/conferences | 10.9 |
| Visit customers/suppliers/businesses | 9.3 |
| Learn Spanish | 12.4 |

Note: Percentages listed total more than 100%, because most visitors participate in several of these activities while in Costa Rica.

*Source: Costa Rican Chamber of Tourism (CANATUR)*

company officials now agree they can only advance technologically through private investment, but the question is how to introduce private enterprise without dismantling an institution that has come to be a regional model.

Trends toward privatization are more advanced in areas such as road construction, food retailing, agricultural products, banking and high technology. The country's economic climate and investment incentives were enough to entice the high-tech giant Intel to open its first Latin American assembly, testing, packaging and export plant here. Costa Rica beat out Mexico, Brazil and Chile for this distinction. The plant is currently under construction and hopes to export its first shipment in early 1998.

**The Tourism Industry**

For years, Costa Rica has been a stable and peaceful base for overseas trade and manufacturing, but the tourism boom in the early 1990s got the word out that the country is also an economical place to live and invest in the vacation industry.

Learning from its mistakes, the government slashed its ridiculously high entry fees to its many national parks. It has also eliminated a 6 percent hotel room tax, which was harshly criticized by the hotel industry since its inception.

The country knows that it needs to improve service and reduce costs to keep the tourist coming back, and it currently seems intent on tourist-friendly policies.

In 1996 more than 800,000 tourists visited Costa Rica, pumping millions into the economy. A recent study revealed that 70 percent are drawn by the country's natural beauty, making it a prime ecotourism destination.

The government has set aside 72 areas as national parks, forest reserves, wildlife refuges or national forest. These regions make up 25 percent of the national territory and contain an astonishing 4 percent of the world's plant, animal and insect species. Costa Rica is a world-renown leader in the preservation of its flora and fauna, although conservationists continue to battle with another of the country's once profitable but now fading industries: timber.

With the exception of the failed Gulf of Papagayo project in the northern province of Guanacaste, which became mired in government graft, favoritism and bureaucracy, the government favors small, eco-friendly tourism that blends with its environment without massively destroying or degrading the rich ecosystem.

This opens the door to the small investor intent on constructing cabinas or small hotels of up to 20 rooms that offer access to activities for which the country is famous, such as jungle tours, white water rafting, deep sea fishing and fauna watching.

The Ministry of Tourism is working closely to chart Costa Rica's touristic course into the future. It has already agreed to:

—Improve and expand the country's main international airport, located near San José. Work is already in progress.
—Channel more funds for improving tourism development.
—Endow the National Training Institute (INA) with more funds for tourism-related programs.
—Improve personal security with more and better trained police, especially downtown and in tourist areas.
—Improve road conditions and signing.

The hotel and bed and breakfast industry, nationwide, is currently experiencing a glut of rooms resulting from the building boom of the early 1990s, but unique lodging is always in demand. Building anything in Costa Rica is bureaucratic and costly due to delays. Before embarking on any construction project, become thoroughly familiar with the country's requirements and consult a good, highly recommended lawyer.

**Manufacturing and Exports**

With investors' sights turned traditionally to the "Asian Tiger" countries and Eastern Europe, many U.S. entrepreneurs are unaware of the enormous growth potential that exists right here in their own back yard.

---

**Latin America Trade Facts**

✓ Consumer markets in Latin America will exceed those of Europe and Japan by 2010.
✓ Europe and Asia can't compete with Latin America's low labor costs.
✓ The region shares a generally "pro U.S." attitude with unmatched proximity by land, sea and air.
✓ Political and commercial risk is considerably less than in Eastern Europe or the former Soviet block countries.
✓ Markets are opening up and an emerging middle class is demanding consumer goods as never before.

---

Small business owners here not only benefit by proximity to the rich U.S. market, but can also take advantage of Costa Rica's regional trade agreements with Panama, Nicaragua, Guatemala, El Salvador, and Honduras. The Central American Common Market already enjoys a collective GDP of $27.7 billion and a population totaling almost 30 million. Costa Rica also has trade agreements with Mexico. These agreements will eventually create a common customs service and permit free movement of labor and capital within the region. Before long the entire Western Hemisphere should be one big trading block.

## *Small Business Options*

Still undecided about what type of business is best for you in Costa Rica? Business opportunities fall into two main categories: Importing, or direct investment in the economy, i.e. tourism, service or exporting. The following list may help narrow the possibilities:

## Importing International Goods

Many entrepreneurs have found their niche importing select, hard-to-find goods from abroad that appeal to Costa Rica's large foreign population and its upper class citizens, who are always on the lookout for articles from abroad.

Literally all of the large supermarkets import certain goods, but the small importer can become more specialized, catering to the refined tastes of the foreign resident who is generally willing to pay more for a quality product from home.

Foreigners who have lived in Costa Rica for years brace themselves for the chorus of "can you bring me?s" that emerge from the mouths of foreign friends when they hear someone is going back home for vacation or business. Can you bring me some horseradish? It won't take up much room in your bag.

### ¡PURA VIDA!

Expat businessman, fresh off the plane and ready to make his first million.

The same businessman returning home broke one year later -- Research? Who needs research?

Can you bring me some bagels? Just a few dozen? Can you bring me some apple butter? Can you bring me some hazelnuts? ...some cookies? ...some computer parts? ...some books?

The clever entrepreneur can capitalize on these wants by importing the hard-to-find goods directly. And the next time a desperate neighbor asks for something, he or she can say, "Sure, just head down to my shop in San José, aisle 3, top shelf. And while you're on your way out, be sure to make a little deposit in my new *cash register*."

A 1993 Commerce Department study of U.S. exporters reported that 96 percent of manufactures that sell goods abroad are small to mid-size, and more than 20,000 manufacturing companies exist with stocks of exportable products that aren't being exported. You can take advantage of those numbers, make a little money and provide a service the foreign community and upscale nationals are clamoring for.

### Direct Investment

The Costa Rican domestic goods and services industry needs you! Come for a few extended visits and determine what you can provide that people — foreign and national — will pay for, whether it be a mail service, messenger service, catering service, quality carpentry, crafts, consulting, tour operating, whatever. And then come on down and do it better than anyone else.

### Tourism

Of the 800,000 visitors that come to Costa Rica, 60 percent come for ecotourism and beaches. More than ever, investors are choosing to "go into business with nature" to capitalize on tourism.

Small cabins or bed and breakfasts of four to 20 rooms have traditionally been popular investments. Beware of the current hotel room glut, however, that is keeping many of the country's hoteliers up nights, wondering how to attract guests. Unique lodging that offers a diverse, natural experience could still pay off for the clever and energetic investor.

That's all the more reason to go into partnership with nature and come up with some new ideas for tours or tourist attractions, such as the new Iguana Farm near the Pacific beach community of Jacó, where tourists can see, touch and learn about this prehistoric lizard. You could also try giving orientation tours to groups of retirees who come to live in Costa Rica for its low cost of living.

**Service Industry**

Regardless of the type of service-sector business you offer, fast, reliable and quality service will keep the customers coming back. Foreign residents and upscale Costa Ricans look for services they've grown accustomed to abroad. They're demanding customers, but can also become lucrative ones for the entrepreneur who can meet their needs.

Look around you. Observe what's successful in your own hometown and then decide if you can adapt the service and market it in Costa Rica.

**Export/Manufacturing**

Costa Rica's pleasant living environment, fine schools, relatively low labor costs, adequate telecommunications and utilities services and friendly people makes it an ideal home base for the small manufacturer or exporter. It's central location provides almost unmatched access to the U.S., Canada and Mexico, as well as Central and South America.

## *FREE TRADE ZONES*

The Free Trade Zone is Costa Rica's premier investment incentive for assembly and manufacturing exports. Resembling modern industrial parks that provide factory space, communications, high-voltage energy and on-site customs, free trade zones are located all over the country.

Companies who invest in Costa Rica under this program are entitled to duty-free import of the raw materials necessary for the manufacturing process, unrestricted revenue repatriation and expedited customs services.

Many companies, particularly in the textile industry, have been operating for years under this system. In the Atlantic slope community of Turrialba, one free zone company manufacturers all the baseballs used in the U.S. Major League teams! For more information about the country's free zone system, call the Costa Rican Coalition for Investment Incentives (CINDE) at Tel: (506) 220-0036, Fax: (506) 220-4754.

## *STARTING TIPS FOR SMALL BUSINESSES*

Many products and services are still needed in Costa Rica. The following tips should help you determine how to successfully find a niche and provide what the market is lacking. But the main key is research.

**Study before you go**  Scan past and present editions of The Tico Times and Costa Rica Today English-language newspapers. The Costa Rican-American Chamber of Commerce (AmCham) can provide a host of books and other helpful information. And you computerphiles, don't forget to "surf the net." Go on-line to research Costa Rica's web pages on the World Wide Web.

**Plan each trip**  Don't move to Costa Rica permanently until you plan several extended travel and research trips here. Set the specific goals of each trip ahead of time, and try to make appointments with key people or business representatives *before* you leave home. Find out what trade groups specialize in your area of interest and contact them before you arrive in-country. Pre-departure planning will make each research trip more productive.

**Follow the Money**  Tourism is the leading source of Costa Rica's foreign revenue. Visit the gift shops, English-language bookstores, hotels, travel agencies, tours and other tourist-related businesses to see if there is any aspect of those businesses that you could provide better -- or start something up that isn't here yet. Discovering what the local market lacks is the best way to determine how to get your foot in the door.

**Don't Forget About the Locals** Costa Rica has large middle and upper classes that don't mind spending extra on products and services that meet their needs and expectations. Imported cosmetics and U.S. quality clothing and "gadgets," such as certain tools, toys, model cars, kitchen supplies and electronics are products the local population wants, but has a hard time finding. Talk to the locals. They'll give you plenty of good ideas.

**Expatriate Markets** More than 20,000 full-time foreign residents live in Costa Rica at least six months out of the year. Hang around the American Legion, Democrats or Republicans Abroad, the Rotary Club or at other popular clubs and organizations to find out what local expat's are longing for.

**New Technology** Costa Rica towers above many of its regional neighbors in computers and technology. Most basic systems and gadgets are already available here, but a plethora of specialized or unusual products could be very popular, but are still unavailable. Keep tabs on the technology back home. Once you're familiar with the local markets, you'll be able to determine what will sell and how to get it here fast to get the jump on the competition. Customs processing and duties will be you biggest challenges.

**Look to the Countryside** The Costa Rican countryside is filled with obscure artisans who have been mastering their craft for years, but have never successfully marketed their products. This may be especially true in the indigenous border regions with Panama and Nicaragua.

If you can latch-on to a reliable and skilled artisan of wicker products, pottery, bamboo furniture, wood carving or other craft, you may be able to generate enough profits for both of you. Take samples of the work back home and show them to popular import dealers. If the product makes the grade, be ready to take an order.

## BEFORE STARTING A BUSINESS

Before investing, you should fully understand the investment climate of Costa Rica. Your best first step should be to contact CINDE, the Costa Rican Investment and Trade Development Board.

CINDE is a private, non-profit institution commissioned to promote and foster social and economic growth in Costa Rica.

Interaction with investors is the key to investment promotion at CINDE. A professional local team is ready to advise on how to do business in Costa Rica along with an office strategically located in Miami. Custom-made itineraries are created according to investor's needs. Follow-up support services that include legal counseling and personnel recruiting make CINDE a true one-stop office. Contact CINDE at (506) 220-0036.

## WANT TO KNOW MORE?

For more information, call the English-language weekly newspaper, **The Tico Times**, for its "Investment Directory," a list of English-speaking persons who will provide specialized investment information (222-0040); the Costa Rican-American Chamber of Commerce (AmCham) at 220-2200 or the government's Center for Promotion of Exports (CENPRO) at 221-7166.

The Costa Rican American Chamber of Commerce (AmCham) is a private non-profit organization founded in 1973. Devoted to the promotion of trade and investment between the United States, Costa Rica and other countries, the very active and highly respected chamber has a membership of 1,200 representatives from nearly 300 of the top companies in Costa Rica.

Services provided by the Chamber include advice on business practices and investing in Costa Rica, marketing and joint venture opportunities, seminars and forums on timely business topics, and monthly luncheons featuring distinguished speakers from the international and Costa Rican business communities.

The chamber publishes the **Guide to Investing and Doing Business in Costa Rica.** Written by the expert's experts, the **Guide** is an invaluable reference tool for potential investors seeking accurate and concise information on the Costa Rican investment environment.

AmCham also publishes a **Glossary of Financial and Accounting Terms,** which contains accurate Spanish/English translations of the modern business vocabulary.

**Business Costa Rica**, AmCham's monthly magazine, provides updated economic information, timely articles on what's news in the local business community, and the latest news from Washington affecting the Costa Rican business climate.

## FOR THE PASSIVE INVESTOR

**Bond Market** If you're a bond investor, be aware that you might not want your money tied up for six months, as devaluation or inflation could erode your gains. A one-to-three month bond investment is perhaps a surer bet.

As of this writing, interest rates on benchmark six-month government bonds are hovering around 22 percent. The central government's fiscal deficit consumed 4.4 percent of the country's gross domestic product (GDP) in 1995, and the same was expected for 1996 at press time. Costa Rica is still experiencing an economic recession, but encouraging statistics indicate that the situation is leveling off. Zero growth was, nevertheless expected for 1996.

The government will continue its policy of daily "mini-devaluations" of the colón to keep pace of international market conditions. Interest rates are expected to remain steady

*Continued on page 132*

## Securities Available in Costa Rica

| TYPES OF SECURITIES | DESCRIPTION | USE OF MONEY | MATURITIES | INTEREST RATE (NET) | |
|---|---|---|---|---|---|
| 1. INVESTMENT CERTIFICATES | Documents representing a company's liability, stating its commitment to pay their par value at maturity. There is a nonspecific guarantee. They are backed only by the prestige of the issuer. | Companies use such resources as working capital. | 30, 60, 90, 180, 360 and up to 1800 days. | 90 days<br>180 days<br>360 days | 21%<br>23%<br>23.50% |
| 2. CERTIFICATES OF DEPOSIT | Certificates issued by the State Banks. They are unconditionally backed by the federal government. | Used by the state banks to finance their operations. | 30, 60, 90, 180, 360 and up to 1800 days. | 30 days<br>60 days<br>90 days<br>180 days | 8.50%<br>14%<br>14%<br>16% |
| 3. MORTGAGE INVESTMENT CERTIFICATES | They represent mortgage rights with the same guarantee. They can be partially or totally transferred by means of mortgage participation contracts documented with "Mortgage Investment Certificates". | Used by mutual companies in order to meet their temporary cash needs. | 30, 60, 90, 180 and 360 days. | 30 days<br>60 days<br>90 days | 26.00%<br>27.50%<br>28.00% |
| 4. REPO'S | A security repurchase agreement (RP) involves the sale of a security together with an agreement to repurchase the security at specified future date and at a price that includes accumulated interest. | This is one of the financing sources of Costa Rican corporations. The security must be registered. | 30, 60, 90, 120, 180, 210 and 360 days. | 30 days<br>60 days<br>90 days<br>180 days | 20.50%<br>21%<br>21%<br>23% |
| 5. BANKERS ACCEPTANCES | Short-term drafts drawn on small or medium-sized companies, and accepted by a banking institution for its own account. They are backed by the solvency of the supporting bank. | To provide small and medium-sized companies with fresh resources. | 30, 60, 90 and 180 days | 30 days<br>60 days<br>90 days<br>180 days | 22%<br>23%<br>23.50%<br>24% |
| 6. MONETARY STABILIZATION BONDS | Bearer securities stating the Federal Government's commitment to pay their par value at maturity. | Monetary regulation. | 30, 60, 90, 180, 360 and up to 1800 days. | 30 days<br>90 days<br>180 days<br>360 days | 22%<br>23%<br>23.50%<br>24% |
| 7. INTERNAL DEBT BONDS | Bearer security stating the Federal Government's commitment to pay their par value at maturity. | Financing of government expenditures. | 30, 60, 90, 180, 360 and up to 1800 days. | 28 days<br>84 days<br>168 days<br>360 days | 18.75%<br>22.15%<br>23.25%<br>23.23% |

*Source: Aldesa Valores Brokerage House and The Tico Times.*

or fall slightly in 1997. To avoid the inflationary tendencies always associated with election year politics, President José María Figures has promised to clamp down on electoral spending and "special allocations" normally granted to politicians for public works projects within their jurisdictions to garner party support from their constituents.

**Stock Market** The new Electronic Stock Exchange opened in April of 1993, quickly adding competition and excitement to the local market.

The Electronic Exchange came about because the existing Costa Rican National Stock Exchange limited participation. Broker commissions ran too high, and the focus shifted too far toward public sector securities and short-term notes.

The Electronic Exchange is an offshoot of the Chilean Electronic Exchange and it's expected to hookup within the next few years to other markets in Central America, Colombia, Argentina and Chile. For more information, contact the Electronic Stock Exchange at 257-2750 or fax at 233-7209.

But don't think the traditional Costa Rican National Stock has been asleep to the competition. It has slashed its broker commissions and is working hard to woo the investors and modernize.

This Exchange was born in 1976 and is now by far the biggest in Central America, trading 741 billion colones (US$5.4 billion), a sum equal to 80 percent of the country's gross national product (GDP). For more information contact 222-8011.

### Tips for Success

*Research, patience, anticipation and acceptance of the culture is the key to success in Costa Rica. Get used to the "Tico" way of doing things. It may take a little getting used to, but once you've been here for a while, you'll find that it's the only way to ultimately get what you need. Neither life nor business here is easy. It's always best to hope for the best, but expect the worst -- and plan for it. When the going gets tough, head to the beach, work on your tan, regroup and get back to it.*

# SMALL BUSINESS START UPS

Foreigners who are not permanent residents of Costa Rica are prohibited by law from owning and operating a business unless they do it as the head of their own Costa Rican corporation (see chapter on Offshore Corporations).

There are several types of corporations; however, the one called "Sociedad Anónima," or "S.A.," has a structure similar to that of corporations in the U.S., and is the most recommended.

This type of company includes a board of directors and a shareholders assembly; its shares can be freely traded in the stock market, or sold or bought directly in a private manner.

The first step is to contact a lawyer —a must in this case— to draft the company charter with characteristics defined by the client.

Once registered, the company can engage in any type of legal business, except for buying state properties or obtaining state concessions. The cost to set up a Costa Rican corporation ranges from $300 to $800.

Foreigners own a wide rage of businesses in Costa Rica, including Bed & Breakfasts, restaurants, tour companies, Spanish schools, import-export companies, consulting firms and more.

Most of these operate as "S.A." corporations that offer wide-open opportunities for the adventurous, persistent entrepreneur.

## THE SMALL BUSINESS OWNER

How frugal can you be? It is vital that anyone starting a small business in Costa Rica keep start-up and operation expenses to a bare minimum.

Costa Rica's low cost of living is probably the micro business person's greatest asset here. A couple can live comfortably, but frugally, on $1,200 per month, including entertainment and housekeeper.

General business start-up costs will probably run about 75 percent lower than in the U.S. or Canada. This will permit you to live well, as your business gets started and revenues grow.

Wise entrepreneurs start small, find their niche and build a company that serves first Costa Rica and then the world.

But, regardless of your prior experience, starting a business here isn't easy. Don't make the mistake in thinking that if you were successful in a developed country like the U.S. or Canada, that creating a new, successful business here will be a "piece of cake." Conduct a thorough feasibility study of your business's prospects before you move here permanently. Not to do so will only cost you more. A lot more.

Any of the successful old timers here will remind you of the adage that is often repeated to the overly confident first timer: *"In order to leave Costa Rica with a million dollars, you first have to come here with two million."* That is, unless you've done your homework.

## AN OVERSEAS BUSINESS IS BORN

Literally all of Costa Rica's most successful entrepreneurs got that way due to their ability to identify local needs and then find a unique way to meet those needs, taking advantage of the country's potential for low-cost business start-up.

To illustrate our point, we'll use the example of "Eddy," a resourceful, if fictitious, newcomer to Costa Rica, who, in spite of his inability to write a decent sentence, went on to become an international publishing baron who now rules his paper-and-ink empire from an oak-paneled office on the fiftieth floor of some highbrow high-rise.

"Eddy's" experiences will give you a good idea about how great ideas born of humble beginnings can and do pay off.

"Eddy" was a successful small businessman when he came to Costa Rica to get away from the hype and hustle of Los Angeles and become his own boss. "Eddy" was amazed by the country's natural beauty, low cost of living and near-perfect weather, but realized that he would have to set up some sort of business if he was going to stay here.

**Always** interested in real estate, and a natural-born salesman, "Eddy" started walking around. He spoke to established members of the foreign business community, including local realtors, builders and architects.

To "get his feet wet" in the new culture, he worked for a short time for a local real estate company, learning the laws, perfecting his rudimentary Spanish, juggling with local bureaucracy and listening to the needs and questions of hundreds of potential buyers and sellers.

It didn't take him long to realize that almost all real estate investors had the same questions, fears and doubts, but couldn't begin confronting those uncertainties until they landed in-country -- and even then, they still found it hard to find the answers.

"Eddy's" entrepreneurial grey matter started churning. He visited local bookstores -- there were plenty of travel, history and cultural publications, but nothing whatsoever about the practical matter of buying real estate in Costa Rica.

"A book! That's it! But wait a minute," thought Eddy. "What do I know about writing a book? Even my own mother tells me she can't make heads or tails of the letters I write to her?" After reading the local English-language newspapers and other publications, Eddy soon realized that talented, native English-speaking writers already lived in Costa Rica. Maybe they'd be interested in helping him.

## ¡PURA VIDA!

The Costa Rican business executive -- from the board room to the beach!

**Marshalling** local talent and using other books he admired as a guide, Eddy used his ample real estate knowledge to create the book's table of contents. He then paid local writers, desperately eking out a living at their own jobs and eager for additional income, to research and write each of the book's chapters.

As he continued walking, talking and "selling" his idea, Eddy discovered that local real estate agencies and related companies enthusiastically supported the book as a means of getting their names out to potential investors.

They agreed to buy advertising. Easing his weary frame into a reception room armchair and staring down at his well-worn shoes, Eddy whipped out his pocket calculator. The advertisements, he discovered excitedly, would completely cover the production costs of the book.

In his travels, Eddy noticed that one writer in particular, we'll call her "Candace," was especially talented, and did graphic design as well. He soon discovered that "Candace" had just created her own Costa Rican corporation and was offering writing, editing and designing services to all.

Candace carefully edited the chapters contributed by local writers and gave them the special touch that Eddy was looking for. She understood that Eddy was just starting out, and charged him special rates at first, carefully banking on Eddy's ample entrepreneurial skills for a hefty future pay off. "A kindred spirit!" thought Eddy. "I think this is the beginning of a profitable relationship." And so it became.

**Now** that Candace was in charge of the book's "quality control," Eddy was freer to concentrate on the dollars and "sense" of his project. After talking with local printers to verify costs, Eddy jotted down his budget and expenses in an old notebook based on the 10 advertisements he had been able to sell for $300 each.

- Printing: $2,000 (1,000 books at $2,00 per book)
- Info supplied by real estate agents: no cost
- Writing and production: $800
- Total cost: $2,800
- Revenues from ad sales: $3,000 (10 x $300)

Even after paying all expenses, Eddy saw he had already made a "profit" of $200. Then he set to work designing a marketing strategy.

He decided that each book would sell for $15.00. He knew from prior research that some 40 of the country's hotels, bookstores and souvenir stands had already agreed to sell the book. Giving them the traditional 30 percent per book sold, Eddy saw that he stood to profit $10.50 per book for a total profit of $10,500 if he sold all 1,000 books.

"I need to sell only 114 books per month to cover my $1,200 monthly living expenses," thought Eddy. "That's only about three books per stand per month!"

To free-up his time to develop other book ideas, Eddy hired a trustworthy young college student to make sure all the points of sale had books in stock. She was also in charge of collecting every month, for which she kept 15 percent of the profits. He had to supervise her closely and continue seeking new stores to sell the book, but after a while she managed collections and distribution on her own.

Eddy sighed with relief. Now that his monthly expenses were covered, he could dedicate himself to bigger and better money-making projects.

**Eddy** continued with this same formula and published an entire series of real estate books covering the countries in Central America and Caribbean.

Clever Candace penned and designed each book from her office in Costa Rica for a price that would have been laughable in the U.S. Eddy branched out and introduced his products into U.S. bookstores, where the customers literally gobbled them up. Candace communicated with the now roving Eddy through e-mail, fax and telephone.

"Eddy," who had trouble writing an intelligible letter to his mom, had become a successful international publisher. "And all it took," thought a reminiscent Eddy, as he leaned back in his leather swivel chair in his fiftieth floor office and lit a fine Cuban stogie, was a good idea, a lot of energy and the ability to locate and utilize top-quality people."

**Sound** unrealistic? Too good to be true? We at OG books are so convinced that this is a profitable idea, that we look forward to buying the first $300 advertisement from the ambitious entrepreneur who puts this real estate book together. We're waiting!

### *OVERSEAS OPPORTUNITIES 2000* ★ ★ ★ ★

The following business ideas are only some of the opportunities that currently exist in Costa Rica for investors of every budget, level of experience and professional background. They are classified based on the approximate minimum start-up capital required: $3,000 or less, $10, 000 or less and more than $10,000.

Remember, in Costa Rica a couple only needs about $1,200 to live comfortably. So what do you think? Got any good ideas?

## START-UPS FOR LESS THAN $3,000

**Resident Application Processor** Budding entrepreneurs have enough on their hands just getting their new business started, without worrying about applying for residency. Most choose to pay a reliable person to do their residency application procedures for them.

Costa Rican lawyers currently charge from $800 to $1,500 for this service, yet it doesn't require a lawyer to do these procedures. A good command of Spanish, or reliable bilingual assistant, is a must, as well as the ability to make important contacts at immigration. Once you learn the ropes, you could even charge half that price -- $400 -- and with only three clients per month, earn enough for a couple to live comfortably. This business literally requires no start-up capital.

**Publishing** Everything is fair game, from tourist and autotrader magazines to nickel ad's and real estate guides. Be creative and get advertising to cover production costs. There are plenty of dance schools in Costa Rica that would pay for an ad in a publication on local dance. Or try printing a coloring book in which local kid-related businesses like fast-food chains and toy stores not only provide the art, but also pay for the privilege of appearing in the book. With this project's advertising potential, you could probably give away the finished books for free and still come out ahead.

**Public Advertising Sign Company** Advertising is popular in Costa Rica. Start a company that offers small billboard advertising in restaurant areas and in public restrooms. Talk with taxi company cooperatives about placing advertising directly on the cabs. A contract with a big multinational here could net you some hefty profits.

**Desktop Publishing/Graphic Arts** As regional markets continue to go global, small companies need creative, articulate people who speak the language of the powerful North American consumer. If you're good with a jingle and have an eye for art, offer your services to small to mid-size companies that are geared toward the expatriate market. Once you develop a loyal clientele, you'll have to hire an assistant to keep up with the work.

**Souvenirs** Room still exists for creative souvenir sales. Think back on your own experiences as a frustrated souvenir shopper. Remember how hard it was to find what you were looking for? You can offer those hard-to-find items at your own shop, or by pushing your wares in other stores.

**Internet Consulting and World Wide Web Page Design** Start a company in this new and dynamic field that targets national and international corporations. Show companies how they can save on long-distance telephone rates by using e-mail and internet phones. This is a rapidly growing field with unlimited potential. Currently, almost everyone who offers this service in Costa Rica is way overpriced.

**Import U.S. quality clothing** Apparel is expensive in Costa Rica and the quality leaves much to be desired. Costa Ricans are very appearance-conscious and will pay more for quality. This could be a good opportunity for someone who is skilled at providing what the customers want at competitive prices.

**Maid Service** Housekeepers are abundant in Costa Rica and work for practically nothing, but honest, reliable, hard-working ones are few and far between. Start a maid service to put middle and upper-class residents and nationals in touch with the good ones. And don't forget the business customer! Small to mid-size companies need cleaning and maintenance people even more than family residences. You could fill the need with your screened and approved "cleaning technicians."

**Distribution Service** Professional, reliable delivery services are in short supply in Costa Rica and could offer opportunity to an individual with a little hustle. Hotels, souvenir shops, bed and breakfasts and other businesses, particularly at the beach, depend heavily on periodic trips to San José to replenish their stocks of snack foods, cosmetics, souvenirs, toiletries and more. You could provide a delivery service for these much-needed articles. This is a hard, tedious business, but the need exists, and where there is need, there is opportunity.

**Second-Hand Dealer** Enough foreigners come and go in Costa Rica that some people make a decent living "trafficking" in household furnishings. These people offer to buy entire households of furniture, clothing and appliances, eliminating the need for those on their way out to advertise and sell off their possessions little by little. These traffickers then sell to those who are looking for bargains on quality furnishings. Place an ad in the local papers that you will pay cash for household furnishings. Then wait for phone calls.

## *START-UPS FOR LESS THAN $10,000* ★ ★ ★ ★

**Private Post Offices** Competition for these businesses, which offer customers access to a U.S. post office box and address, is tough in San José, but what about offering the same service in popular expat coastal communities, such as Manuel Antonio or Flamingo? The Costa Rican national postal service is slow and notorious for theft. This is a good opportunity for someone who can offer full-service mail, packaging, stamps and other options in popular communities outside of the capital.

**Typing and Translation Service** Open a small office providing reliable, quality service that targets the expatriate resident and national and international companies. Translation and interpreter services from Spanish into English and vice versa are in demand in Costa Rica, which often hosts international business, political and financial forums. If you invest in quality equipment, you'll also be eligible for government contracts. It isn't necessary to speak Spanish to establish this type of business, only the ability to put together a good, bilingual staff that will work for low, Costa Rican wages.

**Used Computer Sales and Training** Buy some quality computer equipment second-hand in the U.S. and ship it to Costa Rica to sell on the local market. The country's import tariffs on computer equipment are low because the government doesn't want the country to miss out on the techno-revolution. A large middle and business class is clamoring for low-cost, quality machines. As a complement to your sales, you could also provide technical training to keep your customers up to speed on the latest software and techniques.

**Specialized Tours or Eco Tours** It takes a little creativity to start a tour for less than $10,000, but it can be done. Try taking groups of potential investors or retirees around to show them popular expat and Tico neighborhoods, shopping areas and government buildings. Show them what living in Costa Rica is really like.

At first, you can contract with local transportation companies to haul your customers around. In order to keep the overhead as low as possible. Or, what about motoring people up to the Irazú or Poás volcanoes and then letting them ride back down the hill on mountain bikes?

Go into business with nature! Take small groups to witness the beauty of Nicaragua's beaches or the engineering marvels of the Panama Canal. Natural wonders never fail to amaze visitors and keep them coming back.

**Box Packaging Company** Costa Rica has several private mail services, but none offers a professional packaging service or quality packing materials. Offer a variety of shipping boxes, packing materials, tapes and address labels. This business could be especially profitable around popular gift-giving holidays, such as Christmas or Mother's Day.

**Import Company** Costa Ricans love to eat U.S. foods and wear U.S. clothing. With a sizeable middle and upper class, and a foreign population of 20,000, importers are not hard-pressed to develop a loyal clientele. Try to gain exclusive rights to import some products that can be complemented by a wide range of related products. A good knowledge of Spanish and customs laws will help a lot here.

**Export Company** Costa Rica's exotic hardwoods, tropical foods and unique handicrafts provide unlimited opportunity for export sales to the U.S., Canada and Europe. Costa Rica offers a bevy of incentives to the industrial exporter of goods assembled in-country under the temporary admission system and then exported to the world market. But a clever small-time exporter, with some key contacts abroad, can profit by marketing Costa Rica's native products to the world.

## *START-UPS FROM $10,000 ON UP*

**Gourmet Coffee Shop** Costa Rican's love their coffee, and their tiny country produces some of the world's finest, but coffee is more than just a drink here, it is a national pretext to gather together and socialize.

A creative entrepreneur with a good understanding of the culture could begin a chain of gourmet coffee and snack shops that cater to expats and affluent Costa Ricans. Each location could offer top-quality brew and a congenial meeting place for the country's "in" crowd. This business could be a little expensive to get off the ground, but offers interesting potential.

**Bagel Shop or Bakery** The bagel is a rare object in Costa Rica. Most of the locals don't even know what it is, but love it once they take a bite. A bagel bakery or coffee shop located downtown, in a mall or near popular expatriate areas could become a very popular business.

The shop could also produce bagels on a larger scale for distribution to local supermarkets. Quality bagels will appeal to the expat crowd immediately, but it may take a little while to entice the Ticos.

**Construction Companies** Contractors specializing in steel-frame, tilt-up technology are relatively new here. This type of construction is especially appealing in Costa Rica due to the earthquake resistance it provides. Contractors that provide on-time service with accurate price quotes and good customer service will have the jump on 95 percent of the competition. Finding and training workers in U.S.-style will be the biggest challenge.

**Executive Offices** Deluxe office space for everything from small businesses to multinational corporations could be a lucrative investment, depending on the location and the services offered.

The site should be within easy driving distance of San José and on popular bus routes. Services offered should include translation, telephone answering and message taking, fax and e-mail. The center could cut costs by offering collective secretaries and locating an international courier drop box on-site.

**Food Franchise** Costa Rica has big-name franchises, such as McDonalds, Kentucky Fried Chicken and Pizza Hut, but sandwich shops, doughnut shops and all-night convenience stores are under-represented. U.S. products and foods are popular here and many opportunities exist. Subway opened its first submarine sandwich shop in mid-1995 and currently enjoys a brisk business.

**Arcade and Fun Centers** Costa Rica's young population with a penchant for family life makes the country a prime location for water parks, miniature golf, go-cart tracks, arcades and more. Excellent potential.

**Rental Cabinas** Small, comfortable rental units, popularly called "cabinas," are a favorite business venture for many foreigners living permanently or temporarily in overseas expatriate communities, such as Escazú, in Costa Rica. The foreign owner usually lives in one of the units and rents out the others to fellow expatriates looking for a secure residence. The tenants have access to cooking, cleaning and laundry services. Cabinas rent for $400 to $600 per month, and land sells for $20,000 to $50,000 per acre. The cost to build a small 650 sq. ft. unit would range from $15,000 to $25,000, fully completed.

**Hand Car Wash** Saturday morning in Costa Rica finds literally all car owners out their driveways scrubbing and honing their vehicles to a fine shine. The country offers a few hand wash and vacuum locations, but this could be an interesting opportunity in this car-loving nation.

## A WORD OF CAUTION

Even for an experienced investor, it's a mistake to think that a successful venture in Costa Rica will be easy. It's best to take the Murphy's Law approach and try to anticipate problems before they arise. The only way to do this is through research and extended personal visits before embarking on a major investment.

All business owners will tell you that it takes twice as much money to open a business as they had originally thought, and twice as much time to do some typical daily transactions, such as banking. Research and patience are your best defenses.

Possible obstacles include: faulty or sporadic telephone or electricity service, many national holidays, long bank and post office lines, cumbersome bureaucracy, minimum bank financing, language barriers, culture clashes and finding trustworthy and skilled employees. Talk to everyone you can and do your research before embarking on a new business.

Selected payoffs to certain corrupt government officials may help speed some aspects of a project, but it is specially important that the foreign investor "play by the rules" (See General Information, Pay Off's).

All local tax laws must be followed and proper permits obtained and renewed. It is important to hire the services of a good attorney, skilled in cutting through the red tape. Not to do so will eventually jeopardize your investment.

## *FRANCHISE BUSINESS*

The U.S. franchise industry is a growing international phenomenon that has yet to reach Costa Rica in force. There is still little competition in this region and pay-offs can be high.

Before embarking upon any investment in Costa Rica, do your homework. It's vitally important to find a local business partner with ample business and cultural experience. A trustworthy partner and manager could make the difference between profit and total loss.

Visit the local branch of the American Chamber of Commerce and talk to people in related fields. This will require at least one extended stay in country before start-up can begin. International business expo's and seminars can also provide valuable information. Foreign governments often share a favorable view of franchising because it means revenue and jobs for local people. Advertise in business journals for potential

---

### *Other Business Opportunities Include*

Coin-operated laundry service
Meal trucks
Real estate agents
Occupational health consultants
Used car rentals
Breeding and sale of security dogs
Business consultants

partners, but thoroughly check out a prospective co-investor before signing a contract.

Control of your business is an important factor to consider, especially if you live abroad. Study the market carefully before deciding on a salable product or service. Consider the logistics of quality control, hiring and operation of the business before you invest.

For up-to-date information about international markets, subscribe to an on-line service, such as CompuServe or America Online. But be sure to spend time in the country and do hands-on research. Read the local phone books, get to know the people and the culture, determine your business niche, and then decide if a Costa Rican investment is for you.

## *BUYING AN EXISTING BUSINESS*

Costa Rica doesn't offer the small investor much in the way of already established businesses. Ticos traditionally hand down successful businesses from generation to generation. Micro-businesses, such as neighborhood grocery stores called "pulperías," or other small shops don't usually appeal to the foreign investor, who is more likely to start his or her own business than buy one that's already operating.

If you are determined to purchase an existing business in Costa Rica, first, as always, talk to people who work in similar types of businesses.

They will tell you what the returns are like and will know of others who may consider selling. Local newspapers, such as the English-language Tico Times, and the national daily La Nación, have a "Businesses For Sale" section in their classified ad's, but most people here rely on word-of-mouth contacts.

You can pretty much expect that the accounting books of an existing company for sale will not be up-to-date. Be sure to check with the Direct Taxation Office to make sure the owner owes no back taxes or other liens that you may be responsible for as the business's new owner.

Be extremely wary when buying a corporation here, for many times they include hidden liabilities not listed in the corporate books. A well-recommended and honest attorney will be indispensable. A good rule of thumb? If it seems too good to be true, it probably is.

## *LABOR LAW*

Wages are low in Costa Rica when compared to developed countries (see box in General Information chapter). A factory worker, for instance, earns less than $2.00 per hour.

But beware! The government requires a host of other benefits, including health care, mandatory Christmas bonus and severance pay that increase payroll by about 50 percent per worker. The following list will give you some idea, but it's always best to check with an attorney skilled in the country's complicated labor law.

- Mandatory social security: 22 percent paid by employer and 9 percent deducted from the employee's salary.
- Mandatory accident risk insurance: employer pays 2.5 percent for low-risk employees and 6 to 8 percent or more for high-risk employees.
- Overtime (after 48 hours per week or per contract): an additional 50 percent.
- Night Shift: an additional 50 percent.
- Mandatory holidays: If worked, must be paid as double time. Workers paid on a weekly basis have six holidays per year; employees paid on a monthly basis have 15 holidays per year.
- Mandatory day off: one day per week (if worked, it must be paid double time).
- Mandatory vacation: two weeks for each continuous 50-week period (if worked, must be paid double time).
- Mandatory yearly bonus: one month's pay for every 12 months worked, or the corresponding proportion thereof.

## COSTA RICA ON-LINE

In Costa Rica, *Radiográfica Costarricense* (RACSA), began providing access to the Internet in early 1995. RACSA is a subsidiary of the Costa Rican Electricity Institute (ICE), which enjoys a state-mandated monopoly on telecommunications.

Also protected by the monopoly, RACSA is the country's only provider of on-line computer service, although private services are already jockeying for position in the event the monopoly is lifted. RACSA had 10,000 customers on-line nationwide in 1995. It expects to double that by the end of 1997.

The company promises to deliver a password within 24-hours, but the process could take a week or longer. The $30 monthly fee includes 30 on-line hours. Each additional hour costs $1. For more information contact RACSA, Tel: (506) 287-0087, Fax: (506) 223-1609.

## CYBER CAFÉS

For the computerless among us, Costa Rica offers two "cyber cafés" where "net nuts" can surf the Web by the hour. Both the Café Internet and the Compusource Net Café make e-mail and the net accessible to all. Both charge around $4.00 per hour and serve a great cup of coffee. Call the Café Internet at 231-7368 or the Net Café at 257-4657.

## ON-LINE SERVICES

**On-line Research** International computer on-line services make researching your Latin American investment as easy as switching on a modem and clicking a mouse. A wealth of information about Central and South America is available on "the net," and opportunities exist for those adept at computerized searches. The following is a guide to the main services:

**CompuServe** is the most extensive of the services, offering a wide range of business databases and full access to the Internet. Almost every Latin America country has access. Of particular interest to executives are the International Trade Forum, the Business Database Plus (400 specialty industry newsletters and publications, including The Economist's Business Latin America, The Lagniappe Letter, The Latin America Opportunity Report and others), and the Mexico Forum.

CompuServe has full access to the World Wide Web. For information and free software in the U.S. call 800-609-1674.

**America Online** is the most popular and easy to use of the on-line services. But because it specializes in current publications, its business databases aren't as comprehensive as CompuServe's. There is an international trade discussion group in the Microsoft Small Business Center. For subscription information in the U.S. call 800-827-6364.

**Prodigy** is the easiest to use of the three, but its offerings are limited to current news, weather, U.S. stock information, etc. Its saving grace is the full access it offers for Windows users to the World Wide Web.

**The Internet** is changing faster than up-to-date users' guides can be published.

**The World Wide Web,** often called the "WWW" or simply "the web," is a collection of millions of "home-pages" dedicated to particular topics. The Web stands out among early generations of technology in that it provides sound, text and pictures in an easy-to-use, point-and-click interface. Potential investors in Latin America will find the following Web references useful:

**The Latin American Network Information Center (LANIC)** is the home page of the University of Texas' Center for Latin American Studies.

LANIC contains everything from documents produced by the Latin American and Caribbean Center at Florida International University to regional maps and electronic books about the region. Also available on LANIC is the New Mexico State University Library "Guide to Internet Resources for Latin America." Address: (<http://lanic.utexas.edu/>)

**The Latin American/Spanish WWW & Gopher Services** page will help users find their way to most Web connections in Latin America and other Spanish language services throughout the Internet. Address: (<http://edb518ea.edb.utexas.edu/html/Latin America.html>)

**The National Trade Data Bank**, or NDTB, is a massive database of the U.S. Department of Commerce, which contains reports from U.S. diplomatic missions and commercial officers throughout the region.

NTDB reports offer something for everyone. The "Country Commercial Guides" heading, for example, provides dozens of titles for each country, ranging from analyses of the investment climates and details of trade regulations to lists of the most promising markets and advice for business travelers.

The NDTB also lists contacts at American Chambers of Commerce around the world, has guides for small and medium-sized businesses on basic exporting and trade financing, offers the full text of the North American Free Trade Agreement, and houses other reports, such as the periodic Foreign Labor Trends, and annual reports on economic policy and trade practices. Address: (<http://www.stat-usa.gov>)

**The Intelligence Community Home Page** includes background information on all countries and access to the CIA World Factbook, a useful, if dated, collection of political and economic facts. Address: (<http://www.ic.gov>)

**The International Trade Catalog** is an extensive collection of international trade information, ranging from export hints to NAFTA information to trade policy tools. Address: (<http://www.ces.ncsu.edu/itd.catalog.html>)

**The U.S. Council for International Business** is a gateway to other trade sites on the Web, as well as a storage area for information about import/export documentation. Address: (http://www.uscib.org>)

**The Yahoo Economic Guide** is one of the most popular key-word searchable database of economic and business resources on the Internet.

## COMMERCIAL DATABASES

Although expensive and difficult to operate, nothing tops the big commercial databases for information on Latin America.
**Dialog** (Tel: 800-334-2564) contains thousands of publications covering any subject. However, users can spend hundreds of dollars searching for items sometimes available on CompuServe or the Internet for free.

**InterAm Database for the Americas** (Tel: (602) 622-0925) stores English translations of major Mexican legislation affecting trade and international investors. Also available on CD-ROM, the database is updated regularly with important government decrees, regulations and amendments. Cost: $365/year.

**Latin America Database** (800-472-0888) features news pulled from Latin American media, double-checked for accuracy and synthesized in useful reports on political and economic trends.

Three separate publications are available: The SourceMex weekly report, focusing on economic issues in Mexico; the NotiSur service, with similar reports from South America and the Chronicle of Latin American Economic Affairs. Cost: $110/year for individuals, $565/year for companies.

**Findex** (800-843-7751) is a directory of market research reports, economic analyses and surveys available about countries throughout Latin America. Each report must be ordered and paid for separately. Cost: $105/hour. Available on Dialog.

 ## Tips for Success

### Do's and Don'ts

*After extensively interviewing hundreds of successful foreign business owners in Costa Rica, the staff of OG books came up with the following list of business start-up "do's and don'ts."*

### Do's

....Before you start a business, plan on spending at least three to six months thoroughly researching its potential.
....Try to have a working knowledge of Spanish.
....Be able to live on your savings for about a year and a half, until your new business gets going.
....Start a business that capitalizes on your already existing experience. Costa Rica is a hard place to learn from the ground up.
....Remember that the tourist season in Costa Rica is only six months long (December to May).
....Never let the following words past your lips: "In the U.S., we do it like this..."
....Remember that the more labor-intense your business, the bigger your headache will be.
....Hang out with positive people, not those who are constantly complaining about Costa Rica and its people.

### Don'ts

....Don't trust anyone until you really know them.
....Don't get mixed up with any beer drinking buddies who know of the "perfect" beach lot for sale for a song.
....Don't expect a lot of help from business chambers and

*associations. Costa Rica is like the wild, wild west -- you're on your own.*

*....Don't get in the habit of tipping everyone big, just because everything is so cheap. Before you know it, you'll be tipping your way back home.*

*....Don't think that you can pay everyone off to get the work done faster.*

*....Don't expect business meetings to start on time.*

*....Don't lose your temper over cumbersome bureaucracy -- it will only make matters worse.*

*....Don't take seriously the "fast talker" who appears to have everything figured out. If you've done your research, you already know more anyway.*

*Take a read through our new section, "The People Who've Done It" for case histories of successful foreign entrepreneurs in Costa Rica. They're probably not all that different from you!*

# THE PEOPLE WHO'VE DONE IT

Sure, all you OG books people talk a good piece, but how do we know you're not just handing us a bunch of hooey?

The proof is in the people. Over the years we've met many successful overseas entrepreneurs who have succeeded and prospered according to the OG motto: Start small and then build your business into a national or international contender.

The following pages contain stories of actual people who are living and working in Costa Rica *right now*. Most started their businesses from scratch years ago and today support themselves entirely with their self-generated revenues.

Most live here year-round, having discovered that it is practically impossible to start and maintain a business without staying actively involved in the process. But when they think about the harsh northern weather, the stress and the hassle of life back home, most are perfectly content to remain in the tropical Costa Rican sunshine.

These are some of the people who have "done it," and there are plenty more. Their experiences and secrets to success can provide the potential investor with insight into the daily trials, tribulations and rewards of living and working in Costa Rica.

Read their profiles carefully and learn from their experiences. If you manage to start and maintain a successful business in Costa Rica, it probably won't be long before OG books comes knocking on your door too.

## Investment Consulting

**Name:** Tomás Ghormley

**From:** Rolling Hills, CA

**Residence:** Escazú, 10 yrs.

**Business Name(s):** Anacapa Pacífica, Rancho Buenaventura S.A., Rancho Playa Negra and Anacapa Surf.

**Business Description:** We develop communities on the beaches of the northern province of Guanacaste, purchase and manage properties for investors, and import and manufacture several major brands of surfwear and gear, including Jamaican Style, Scorpion Bay, Free Style and Tavarua.

**Why Costa Rica?:** I first came to surf in 1979 and fell in love with the country. I returned every year for vacation until I finally moved here in 1982.

**Key to Success:** While working in Costa Rica with the U.S. Peace Corps and later with the Agency for International Development (U.S. AID), I learned the importance of true cultural sensitivity. In Costa Rica it is important to understand where someone is coming from and what his or her personal agenda is. The ideal is always a win-win situation. The key in Costa Rica is to understand how to make that happen long-term. You must truly identify with the country and its people, so that your goals help achieve long-term benefits.

## Video Sales and Rental

**Name:** Brett Moar

**From:** BC, Canada

**Residence:** Escazú, 9 yrs.

**Business Name(s):** Video de las Americas and Galería de las Americas.

**Business Description:** We were the first video store in Costa Rica when we opened in 1989. We still have the country's largest selection of videos.

**Why Costa Rica?:** I came with my family looking for a nice place to live and start a business. We originally planned to start a satellite dish business, but the permit process took so long, we decided to open a video store and art gallery.

**Key to Success:** We consistently offer our members the latest video releases from the U.S. We also offer titles that other stores don't.

## Book & Gift Store

**Name:** Angel & Rini Bakx

**From:** Canada & Holland

**Residence:** Heredia, 2 1/2 years

**Business Name(s):** Book Traders

**Business Description:** We buy, sell and trade new and used books, mostly in English, and offer a huge variety of magazines, postcards, souvenirs, t-shirts, unique Costa Rican art and Cuban cigars. The coffee's fresh and hot, the chairs are comfortable and the conversation is always interesting.

**Why Costa Rica?:** We came as newlyweds to start a business. We first thought of maybe a bar or coffee shop, but then we discovered that Book Traders was for sale and had a lot of potential.

**Key to Success:** We listen to our customers, get them what they need and pride ourselves on personalized service. Our plan is to create a full-service smoke shop and comfortable lounge to provide an oasis in the heart of San José from the hustle and bustle of the city.

## Insurance Agency

**Name:** David Garrett

**From:** Uruguay & Mexico

**Residence:** Escazú, 20 yrs.

**Business Name(s):** Garrett & Associates

**Business Description:** We are insurance agents who sell all types of policies for the government monopoly insurance company.

**Why Costa Rica?:** To get out of the rat race.

**Key to Success:** Because the National Insurance Institute (INS) is a government monopoly, its products tend to be outdated and different from what people from other countries expect. We explain the nuances of the system and advise people in English in order to prevent false expectations. As much as possible, we also help clients wade through the red tape.

## Real Estate Sales

**Name:** Lester E. Núñez

**From:** Victoria, BC

**Residence:** Escazú, 1 yr.

**Business Name(s):** Remax Asfia S.A. Real Estate Co.

**Business Description:** Costa Rica's first true franchise real estate company offering buyers and sellers immediate response and access to world-wide connections with more than 2,720 offices and 44,158 associates in more than 16 countries.

**Why Costa Rica?:** To experience a new Latin American culture, for the weather and for the availability of proper health care.

**Key to Success:** Service, service and service, followed by professionalism and integrity, just like North Americans are accustomed to back home. Our service has also earned us a reputation among the local community as an agency on which they can rely and trust throughout the entire real estate process.

# Construction

**Name:** Richard Godfrey

**From:** Chicago

**Residence:** Escazú, 6 yrs.

**Business Name(s):** Gyp-Tech

**Business Description:** We import, sell and install drywall, metal framing and other building materials, with specialties in "turn key" home construction.

**Why Costa Rica?:** I'm here to use my knowledge of construction to capitalize on the building opportunities. In Costa Rica you can start and expand a business faster and in a shorter period of time than in the U.S.

**Key to Success:** The advantage of gaining extensive experience in the States and specializing in modern building technologies that have yet to arrive in Costa Rica.

## Attorney at Law

**Name:** Ronald "Blair" Houston

**From:** Vancouver, BC

**Residence:** Escazú, 22 yrs.

**Business Name(s):** Bufete Houston & Asociados

**Business Description:** Law office with specialties in commercial and civil law, real estate, corporate law and investment.

**Why Costa Rica?:** A work offer and adventure brought me to Costa Rica. At 21, I went to work for a Canadian/Costa Rican company involved in forestry, cattle ranching and tourism. During those eight-and-a-half years I spent a lot of time helping the corporation with legal matters and dealing with local lawyers. I saw the opportunity to start a top notch law office serving the expatriate community.

**Key to Success:** We've consistently provided the foreigner with a good, basic understanding of Costa Rican law and what they need "legally" when they start and operate a business and buy or sell real estate or other investments.

## Radio Disk Jockey

**Name:** Joseph Azzara

**From:** San Diego, CA

**Residence:** Rohrmoser, 2 yrs.

**Business Name(s):** Professional disk jockey and real estate agent.

**Business Description:** Between 6 a.m. and 9 a.m., Monday through Friday I become "Joseph King" on Costa Rica's popular bilingual station, Radio Dos -- an established local FM station that watched its ratings go from nowhere to one of the best for its new English-language morning show, playing adult contemporary music. I'm also a realtor with Remax Centro Real Estate Co.

**Why Costa Rica?:** For a new start on life and to be a "big fish in a little pond."

**Key to Success:** Patience, understanding and acceptance of another culture and a healthy respect for the people. I feel I've done well here, in part, because I don't try to influence anyone to change to North American ways, but work side by side with Costa Ricans for the benefit of all.

## Writing & Graphic Design

### *GONE TO THE BEACH!*

**Name:** Christine Pratt

**From:** Portland, OR

**Residence:** Pavas, 7 yrs.

**Business Name(s):** Red Bicycle Communications S.A.

**Business Description:** Professional newswriting, ad copy writing, editing and graphic design in English or Spanish, along with guaranteed trouble-free commercial printing.

**Why Costa Rica?:** Spanish, gallo pinto, ranchera music, coffee hour, the churros at Manolo's, San José on a Sunday afternoon, bus names, cool sunshine, chivalrous men, kids, conversation, La Sabana park, the campo, coffee picking, humble generosity and beer with bocas.

**Key to Success:** The best service in town. I give my customers what they want without subjecting them to the stress, problems and delays associated with design, printing and advertising. On a personal level, I think I fit in well here because I genuinely like it. I respect Costa Ricans, have learned a lot from them and love being with them.

## Irrigation and Drainage

**Name:** Chuck Turner

**From:** Davenport, Iowa & Fort Lauderdale, FL.

**Residence:** Escazú, 26 yrs.

**Business Name(s):** Dragas & Gruas S.A.

**Business Description:** I'm a contractor for dragline work. Most of my business has been with banana plantations on the Atlantic. This work entails cleaning up the debris and erosion of rivers and excavating primary and secondary canals for drainage systems.

**Why Costa Rica?:** It was originally the idea of my father, who visited Costa Rica several times in the late 1960s and often spoke of the potential that exists.

**Key to Success:** Becoming part of the system and accepting a different culture, which often does not coincide with your family background. Patience, prudence and perseverance are required to live happily in Costa Rica. Enjoy the good things the country has to offer -- great climate, natural beauty and friendly people. Go native, and make Costa Ricans your best friends.

# BANKING

Going to the bank? Make sure you bring along some good reading material. Costa Rica's banks were socialized after the 1948 revolution, and literally all still use many of the paper-pushing, mechanical procedures of yesteryear. But times are changing.

The tendency to privatize and improve customer service is finally taking hold. The State system is still plagued by inefficiency and long waiting lines, but sweeping reforms of the country's bank law now allows private banks, for the first time in 50 years, to offer checking and savings accounts and have access to Central Bank funds, placing them on nearly equal footing with their big State counterparts.

The Costa Rican government guarantees all monies deposited in its four State banks, which are the Banco Nacional de Costa Rica (BNCR), Banco de Costa Rica (BCR), Banco de Crédito Agrícola de Cartago (BCAC) and Banco Popular; this has contributed to the reputation of stability and dependability earned by the State banks over the years.

Probably the most notable indication of the banking system's stability was the government's handling of the nation's biggest banking crisis in its history — the failure of the Banco Anglo Costarricense in 1994. Government officials assured depositors that they wouldn't lose a cent — and not one did. This helped stabilize confidence in the entire system and prevented huge runs.

This past year revealed a series of favoritism and corruption scandals that touched all of the State banks, including the international entity the Banco Internacional de Costa Rica (BICSA). In nearly every case, the big banks apparently granted loans to non-qualifying borrowers, or permitted certain debtors to overdraw their accounts, sometimes for millions of dollars in loss. Recipients of such bank "favors" were mainly private corporations, but even the country's two main political parties appear to have been recipients of these funds.

In every case, however, the government, though its banking regulatory board, the Superintendency General of Financial Entities (SUGEF), launched full-scale investigations that were conducted in a relatively public manner. The system remains stable and enjoys a high level of public confidence.

The government is currently in the process of selling BICSA, and rumors indicate that the BCR and the BCAC may also soon go on the block.

Aside from the "big four" State banks, the government runs two other specialty banks — the Banco Hipotecario de la Vivienda (BANHVI) for housing and Banco Popular y de Desarrollo Comunal for community development.

The nation has at least 23 private banks and more than 70 financial houses. Only some of these entities have guarantees or insurance from the government. In order to verify claims of such, call the SUGEF at 233-4233.

Leading local economists and bankers predict that the opening up of the country's banking services will soon lead to mergers among smaller banks to fortify their infrastructure, improve their services and give the big State banks "a run for their money." However, these smaller and much more agile and efficient institutions will still be hard-pressed to offer the expensive network of provincial offices that the State banks have operated for years.

## *BANK REFORMS USHER IN EFFICIENCY*

In spite of tenacious resistance by the opposition Social Christian Unity Party (PUSC), President José María Figueres made a watershed decision in late 1995 to break the 47-year national banking monopoly in exchange for vital PUSC support of his tough new tax plan.

For the citizen and foreign resident, this translates into a wider variety of services, including expanded automatic teller machines, debit cards, competitive checking and savings accounts, bank accounts for tourists, the ability to change dollars at any institution and the possibility of drawing-up domestic contracts in foreign currencies.

Under the new policy, exporters are no longer required to exchange 20 percent of their dollar earnings in the state banking system, instead, they merely report their earnings to the Central Bank. Companies will have access to more banks with efficient handling of payroll checks.

Check cashing will also be streamlined. The new law requires banks to exchange domestic checks within one work day. Previously banks were known to float checks for up to three weeks.

In exchange for these benefits, private banks must either provide 17 percent of their capital at discounted loan rates to public banks to facilitate development projects, or open four branches in rural areas.

Keep in mind the *future* tense of the last few paragraphs. Competition and privatization *are expected* to lead to more efficiency, but before venturing into a State bank, it is still necessary to arm yourself with patience and a good book.

## *BANK SERVICES*

Most of the state and private banks offer 24-hour automatic tellers that will dispense up to ¢50,000 ($230) at a time from your checking or savings account.

To obtain checking and savings accounts, the bank requires the recommendations of at least two people who do business with the bank. This is obviously a pain in the neck for anyone who has just arrived in the country, but be creative!

Banks also offer Certificates of Deposit in colones or U.S. dollars. No interest is accrued after the expiration date.

Depositors of large sums of money should be aware that many of the banks pay interest on the lowest amount of money in the account for that month.

For example, if you deposit $10,000 on the fifth of the month into your account that has a current balance of $100, the bank will pay the monthly interest based on that $100. The $10,000 will not begin accruing interest until the following month.

Thievery such as this has jeopardized the country's national banking system in international circles. A better idea is to keep as little money as possible in your savings account and buy certificates of deposit, which pay much better interest.

## *CREDIT*

At most state-owned banks, obtaining loans is also difficult for most foreigners, who generally don't want the credit once they see the interest rates in the 25 percent range. Visa and Mastercard accounts are also offered through the national company Credomatic. Credit rates at department and specialty stores are always outrageous — from 30 percent all the way up to 110 percent!

## *¡PURA VIDA!*

Oh! Time for coffee! The customers can wait -- anyway, look how they're reading books and talking among themselves. They'll never notice we're gone.

It's not a good idea to hold all your chips in one place. One highly recommended suggestion is to keep enough funds in a federally insured U.S. bank to make you feel secure in case anything happens to your bank here.

There are an estimated 70 financial companies in Costa Rica. They offer many of the same services as private banks and act as markets to obtain working capital and general financial resources. They should be registered with the General Superintendancy of Financial Entities (SUGEF).

Credit cards in dollars are readily accepted in most establishments. Be aware that credit card companies use exchange rates highly favorable to them and not to you, the client. A credit card is, nevertheless, handy for emergencies and for those who don't want to carry a lot of bills around.

For information, contact Credomatic, which carries Visa and MasterCard (253-7744 or 233-2156), Unicard (222-9622); the American Express Travel Service Representative (233-0044); Diners Club (257-6868, Fax: 223-6328); or Visa (223-2211).

### Tips for Success

*Before setting up in Costa Rica, be sure to discuss your plans with your local bank.*

> *•How will you pay your current bills? Some banks make arrangements to transfer funds from a savings to checking account to cover outstanding debts. In other cases, you may arrange to have your creditors send the bill to you in Costa Rica via your private post office box.*

> *•Before you leave home, increase the limit on your credit cards and apply for a personal loan line of credit. You never know if you'll need the money, and it's much easier to arrange this before you leave.*

•*Make arrangements for your bank to wire money to you at a later date, just in case you need it.*

*REMEMBER The best way to protect your money abroad is to leave the bulk of it in an account with an insured bank back home. Only bring/transfer into Costa Rica the money you'll need to live on, and deposit it in a dollar account in one of the local banks.*

*Costa Rican banks with branches in the U.S. include BICSA, Tel: (506) 257-0885 and Banco BFA, Tel: (506) 289-4554.*

## TO AVOID THE LINES

•*Every public and private worker in Costa Rica is paid on the 15th and 30th of every month. These dates are the worst ones to plan daily banking, unless you can arrive at the bank shortly after it opens (usually around 9 a.m.).*

•*Open an account at a money exchange house, or "casa de cambio." You can cash checks there, as well as transfer money without the typical bank bureaucracy. And most tellers speak English.*

•*Each State institution's main branch always offers faster services than its neighborhood satellite offices. Even so, try to arrive in the morning, just as the bank opens.*

•*Services at Costa Rican banks are not centralized. That means you have to stand in one line to cash a check, another to deposit or withdraw from a savings account, and another to buy traveler's checks or other banking transactions. Before waiting in any line, ask at least two people to make sure it's the right one.*

# TAXES

The tax system in Costa Rica is less complex than in other countries but must not be taken lightly.

With the dwindling of international aid, the government now realizes that the only way it can continue to provide the quality health care and labor benefits its citizens have come to expect is through better taxation and collections.

Over the past two years, many businesses have been shut down by judicial order for cheating on their taxes. If anything, the situation should become even more strict in the future, with heavy fines and prison sentences imposed on tax evaders.

The Income Tax Law has become much more complex, and top-quality tax counseling is highly recommended.

## INCOME TAX

Foreign source income is exempt from taxation in Costa Rican. All individuals and business enterprises residing in Costa Rica are subject to tax on income earned in the country. Nonresidents are subject to pay tax on property or business income derived from sources in Costa Rica.

Tax is payable on net income, described by the law as the difference between gross income and allowable deductions.

## A TAX HAVEN?

Costa Rican legislation has always created favorable tax conditions for offshore operations, but the country's popular-

# TAX RATES
## IN COSTA RICA

**Current tax rates for salaried employees, employer's contribution to the government**

| | |
|---|---|
| From ₡0 to ₡153,000 | EXEMPT |
| From ₡153,000 to ₡197,000 | 10% per month |
| More than ₡230,000 | 15% per month |

**Current tax rates for the self-employed**

| | |
|---|---|
| From ₡0 to ₡580,000 | EXEMPT |
| From ₡580,001 to ₡868,000 | 10% per year |
| From ₡868,001 to ₡3,600,000 | 15% per year |
| From ₡3,600,001 to ₡5,400,000 | 20% per year |
| More than ₡5,400,000 | 25% per year |

**Current tax rates for small companies**

Requirement: Gross income in the fiscal period of no more than ₡17,500,000

From ₡0 to ₡8,700,000 of gross income, 10% over profits.

More than ₡8,700,000 up to ₡17,500,000, 20% over profits

ity as such has only caught on over the last few years.

Banks are required by law to maintain absolute secrecy regarding the operations of their clients. Information about normal banking operations is not passed on to any government agency -- including the Tax Department. The Central Bank, however, is privy to such data.

The preceding applies also to any information given to local attorneys, which is completely protected by professional secrecy.

The Tax Information Exchange Agreement between Costa Rica and the United States took effect in February 1991. This agreement allows the exchange of banking information between the two countries, but such an exchange will only occur with express authorization of a Costa Rican judge. The exchange will only be permitted if it relates to a possible tax fraud matter as defined by Costa Rican law.

To date, there have been very few, if any, requests from the U.S. for Costa Rican tax information.

## *CAPITAL GAINS TAX*

No capital gains taxes on real estate exist. However, the Income Tax Law establishes a conveyance tax, at a single rate of 3 percent of properties valued above ₡600,000.

## *SALES TAX*

The sales tax is levied on the sale of products or articles, as well as services rendered in restaurants, bars, hotels, auto repair shops, telephones, photo development shops and many others. The tariff is 15 percent.

## *VEHICLES TAX*

A vehicle ownership tax is paid every year on all vehicles on file at the National Vehicle Registry. The rate varies according to the vehicle's weight and value taken from a list published by the government every January 1.

## *EXPATRIATES FACE SAME TAX LAWS - WITH EXCEPTIONS*

All U.S. citizens, no matter where in the world they live, are subject to the same tax laws as the neighbors they left behind in the U.S.

However, there are some important exceptions. The first is that the U.S. government grants a $70,000 exemption on earned income. To receive this exemption, you must be out of the States for 330 days in a 365 day period.

It is important to note that this is not a deduction, credit or deferral. *It is an outright tax exclusion for those who live outside the U.S.*

If you work overseas and maintain a place of residence in the United States, your tax home is not outside the United States. In other words, to qualify for the foreign-earned-income exclusion, you have to establish both your place of business and your residence outside the United States. *You need to sell or rent your U.S. home and establish a primary residence outside the United States.*

If you meet the following requirements, the U.S. Internal Revenue Service (IRS) will consider you a legitimate foreign resident who qualifies for the $70,000 exemption on earned income.

**Local involvement:** You should show involvement in local social and community activities to the same extent you were involved in such activities in the United States.

**Personal belongings:** The more you take to the foreign country, the more you are seen as establishing a foreign residence.

**Local documents:** It is helpful to obtain a foreign driver's license and foreign voter registration when possible.

**Sleeping quarters:** A transient is more likely to sleep

in a hotel; a resident likely owns housing or signs at least a year-long lease.

**U.S. property:** Owning a vacant U.S. residence is a sign of an intention not to establish a foreign residence. You must sell or rent your U.S. residence to qualify.

**Foreign taxes:** This is the most important consideration for anyone trying to qualify for the foreign-earned-income exclusion. Foreign countries tax on the basis of residence. If you claim exemption from local taxes because you are not a resident of that country, the IRS will conclude that you are a U.S. resident and do not qualify for the foreign-earned-income exclusion under the foreign-residence test.

The $70,000 limit applies to individual single taxpayers. If you are married, you and your spouse potentially can exclude up to $140,000 of foreign-earned income. But you cannot share each other's limit. For example, if one of you earns $85,000 and the other earns $35,000, you exclude only $105,000 on the return ($70,000 plus $35,000).

Remember, to get the exemption *you must file a tax return and claim the exemption on Form 2555.* The IRS has had success in recent years contending that anyone who does not file the return loses the benefit even if he or she meets other requirements.

This exemption does not apply to dividends, pensions and other similar forms of earnings. U.S. residents here have loudly complained about being taxed on their pensions.

If you pay taxes to a foreign country, those taxes can be exempted from your U.S. taxes.

Even if you receive no income in Costa Rica, it is still very important to file the standard tax form 1040. If you live here for a number of years and then decide to return to the United States, it looks highly suspicious if you haven't filed a return in a long time.

Tax forms are available at the U.S. Embassy, 220-3939,

and several U.S. tax experts offer consulting service from right here in Costa Rica. One of the most experienced is Robert E. McBeath. Give him a call at (506) 289-7249.

### Tips for Success

*An ambitious plan to improve tax collection was implemented in 1995. The government can now shut down tax dodgers and throw the owners in prison for up to 10 years. Fines are now imposed on tax dodgers and on those who refuse to give tax inspectors access to the books.*

*Foreigners may be the targets of special scrutiny. Many Costa Ricans don't follow the correct procedures, but OG books strongly advises that all foreigners play by the rules.*

## ¡PURA VIDA!

*Office Essentials*

Professional Attire · Cellular phone · Briefcase with Notepad and Lunch · Beeper · Laptop Computer with Internet Access and Fax Service · Good Signage

# OFFSHORE CORPORATIONS

Offshore corporations sound exotic and full of intrigue, but in Costa Rica, starting one is as easy as baking an apple pie.

Under Costa Rican law, there are three types of legal entities that offer limited liability to their shareholders. These are the Limited Partnership (Sociedad en Comandita), the Limited Liability Company (Sociedad de Responsabilidad Limitada), and the Corporation (Sociedad Anónima), which is the most recommended.

Of the three, the corporation, usually identified by its initials in Spanish, "S.A.," is by far the most widely used. Almost any lawyer will fill out the requisite paperwork, charging anywhere from $300 to $800. The entire process takes about two months. To obtain a reputable, English-speaking lawyer, contact the Costa Rican-American Chamber of Commerce at 220-2200, the U.S. Embassy at 220-3939, or read the chapter, "Finding a Good Lawyer."

The corporation must have a three-member board of directors. Board members are not subject to nationality or residence requirements. The most common practice is to name a president, vice-president, treasurer and secretary.

One of the advantages of owning a corporation (S.A.) is avoiding problems with wills or probates. For example, if you purchase property in the name of a corporation in which you and your spouse are president and vice-president, and the remaining board positions are filled by your children, your property will not be subject to the lengthy probate process in the event of the president's death -- the next-of-kin will simply assume control rather easily.

The U.S. government will not tax the foreign profits generated by the Costa Rican corporation; the Costa Rican government will tax this income, however.

Your Costa Rican accountant will help you deal with these "taxing" matters.

---

### Why a foreigner should own a Costa Rican corporation

Anyone may set up a Costa Rican corporation, whether or not legal residency has been acquired.

- Non-resident foreigners must have a corporation in order to own a business in Costa Rica.
- Real estate in the name of a corporation pays no transfer tax or stamps when it's sold, only legal fees.
- Corporations are liable for vehicles registered in their name. This helps protect you personally from law suits in case of traffic accidents in which the corporate vehicle is at fault.
- Homes or businesses in the name of a corporation are protected from judgement liens or attachments in the event of a law suit.
- Checking or savings accounts in the name of a corporation can offer anonymity.

---

## *PRIVACY*

Investors should be aware that "offshore corporations" in Costa Rica do not provide the same secrecy as in Panama, the Cayman Islands and other shelters. Any Costa Rican or foreigner can go into the Public Registry and find out who are the "legal representatives" of a company, making it difficult to hide from the U.S. Internal Revenue Service.

Now, you'll notice that we said the "legal representatives." Costa Rica's corporation law does allow for the "owner" to remain anonymous, if he or she chooses.

Total anonymity is achieved by appointing a friend, relative or even your attorney as the legal representatives of the corporation. It is important that the board of directors comprise people of confidence, because they have the right to make decisions, buy and sell real estate, hire and fire employees and otherwise act on behalf of the corporation's "real owner."

The "real owner" is the person whose name is on the stock certificates, which should be tucked away in a safety deposit box or another secure place. This person's name need not appear in any of the corporation's legal books.

To ensure that the "real owner" is protected from his or her "straw" board of directors, restrictions should be placed on the board's ability to act. In this way, risk is limited.

Local attorneys recommend that the "real owner" also be a member of the corporation's board of directors as a legal representative to discourage problems that may arise over decision-making power.

If you're looking for a true "anonymous" corporation, most Costa Rican attorneys recommend you take a 30-minute flight to Panama, where corporate law allows for total privacy.

However, the IRS will probably not come looking for most small fry. And the Public Registry doesn't yet have a data bank capable of plugging "norteamericano" into the search button and pulling out the names of U.S. citizens with corporations in Costa Rica.

## *PRIVACY AND TAX LAWS*

Any U.S. citizen should know that while funds can be hidden in Costa Rica, and the U.S. government has not been known to target U.S. citizens living here, the U.S.

government does require certain tax forms to be filed, such as form 5471.

U.S. citizens with more than 5 percent stock in a company are required to file. These requirements extend into a range of areas. For example, taxes must be paid if more than 60 percent of the corporation's income is from passive, investment-type income, such as interest, dividends, annuities, rent, etc.

It's always best to check with your U.S. tax expert and your Costa Rican lawyer on this area.

 Tips for Success

*Creating a Costa Rican corporation for the reasons previously stated is well worth the money, but remember to do everything by the book.*

*Non-resident foreigners must own a Costa Rican corporation to obtain officially registered business receipts for recording sales transactions. The government uses the registration process for tax-collection purposes, and many customers will not accept an unofficial invoice.*

**¡PURA VIDA!**

*Dress for Success*

*San Jose, California*

*San Jose, Costa Rica*

# FINDING A GOOD LAWYER

In Costa Rica, a reliable attorney is the best asset you'll ever acquire for establishing a business, buying or selling real estate, seeking residency status or getting involved in any other investment activity.

National law requires that a notary, who must also be a registered attorney, draw up the documents and make the necessary notations for the legal transfer of real estate. Notaries are also indispensable when forming a Costa Rican corporation -- handy for buying and selling real estate or vehicles.

The Costa Rican legal system is based on Roman Law, and as such, it differs from the U.S. system. A reputable attorney already understands the complexities of the system and can assist you with legal matters in general.

Unless you have an excellent command of Spanish, it is advisable to find a bilingual (Spanish-English) lawyer -- preferably one who has a bilingual secretary -- in order to avoid communication problems and misunderstandings.

Always keep in close contact with your attorney, but never trust him or her completely. It's a good idea to familiarize yourself with the country's legal procedures and transactions that apply to you. Such knowledge goes a long way toward hurrying the attorneys along and keeping them honest.

Legal fees are more affordable in Costa Rica, and with registered attorneys almost outnumbering the country's myriad tropical insects, finding one who meets your needs shouldn't be overly difficult.

Minimum fees are established by the Attorneys Association, but literally all lawyers charge more. Some transactions, such as transferring ownership of real estate or buying a car, are set by a fixed percentage of the amount of the transaction. Most attorneys who deal with foreigners and handle transactions involving investigations, counseling or negotiations, charge between $40.00 to $150.00 per hour.

As a service to our readers we would like to recommend the following attorneys whom we know to be experienced, hard-working and happy to help you:

**Bufete Kanes & Molina Associates, Levie Kanes N., President**
Calle 17, Av. 8-10, No. 845, San José, Costa Rica
**Tel:** (506) 257-5352, 257-5620, **Fax:** (506) 257-7385
**Languages Spoken:** English, Spanish, French, Dutch, German
**Specialty:** Investment, real estate, corporate law, contracts, tourism law, reforestation, international business transactions.

**Carlos S. Fernández Velez**
Calle 33, Av. 8-10, No. 837, San José, Costa Rica
**Tel:** (506) 283-3792, Fax: (506) 234-9159
**Mailing Address:** PO Box 5357-1000 San José, Costa Rica
**Languages Spoken:** Spanish, English
**Speciality:** Residency, pensionado, rentistas, investors and corporations.

**Goldy Ponchner Geller**
Calle 25, Av. 8-10, No. 854, San José, Costa Rica
**Tel:** (506) 256-2601, 232-2578, Fax: (506) 290-5201
**Mailing Address:** PO Box 913-1007 San José, Costa Rica
**Specialty:** Real estate, taxes, immigration, corporations, leases, litigations, contracts and general business law.

**R. Blair Houston**
**Buffete Houston y Asociados**
Calle 36, Av. 7-9, 500 meters north of Toyota, Paseo Colón

San José, Costa Rica
**Tel:** (506) 255-0831, **Fax:** (506) 221-3594
**Languages spoken:** English and Spanish
**Specialties:** Real estate, contracts and corporate law, investments, residency, 20 years' business experience in Costa Rica, studies in business administration in Canada.

**Bufete Odio, Weisleder & Asociados; Sergio Sancho Hernández; Adrian Alvarenga; Jaime Welsledger**
Mailing Address: Apdo. 403-2070 San José, Costa Rica
**Tel:** (506) 222-1721, 221-0580
**Fax:** (506) 222-5589
**Languages spoken:** English, Spanish, French
**Specialty:** International and commercial law, trade marks, investments, real estate, corporate law.

### Tips for Success

*It always takes three or four tries to find a lawyer with whom you feel comfortable. But if there's anything Costa Rica has a surplus of, it's attorneys! Always meet with several who come recommended by reliable sources before you decide who will handle your important personal and business transactions.*

# RESIDENCY

Many first-time visitors to Costa Rica fall in love with the beautiful countryside, perfect climate and friendly people. And on the basis of this first impression, they decide to move here -- just like that!

The idea of living in Costa Rica as a retiree or foreign investor is alluring for many good reasons. The climate is pleasant and warm. The cost of living is lower. A large and friendly foreign community, as well as the Ticos themselves, offer opportunities for new relationships and adventures.

But as tropical and beautiful as the country is, life here will remind you on a daily basis that this isn't paradise!

Rein-in those romantic, impulsive emotions -- at least for a little while -- and don't sell the house, say good-bye to the neighbors and make the move until you've spent at least one extended visit here.

These visits will give you a true taste of Costa Rican life. They will help you determine if you can live with the Spanish language, hour-long waits at the bank, hazardous driving and road conditions and miles of red tape.

Rent an apartment or an "apartotel" and check out real estate prices, shop in the grocery stores, take taxis and buses around town. Talk to foreigners who live here -- you'll find them in language schools, and at the meeting places listed in the chapter on clubs and groups. An excellent way to introduce yourself to Costa Rica is to take a month-long language course and stay with a family. That way you'll get to know foreigners and Ticos.

The foreign community here —and this includes Europeans and Latin Americans as well as North Americans— is fairly large. Some 2,800 pensionados and rentistas live in Costa Rica, along with some 17,000 business owners, foreign government workers and people staying here as perpetual tourists. Ticos themselves are very friendly and polite, but it takes a long time to get to know them well. Social events tend to focus on the family. Like everything else in Costa Rica, deep friendships take time and patience.

## *CULTURE SHOCK*

Even if you adjust well to new situations, you will probably experience some culture shock. L. Robert Kohls' book, *Survival Kit for Overseas Living,* defines culture shock as "the more pronounced reactions to the psychological disorientation most people experience when they move for an extended period of time into a culture markedly different from their own." Symptoms of culture shock include hyper-irritability, bitterness, resentment, homesickness, and depression.

Kohls recommends going back over the reasons you came to the new country in the first place. Then look for logical reasons behind the things you find strange, confusing or threatening.

We at OG Books find that the following are the most common reasons why foreigners move to Costa Rica:

- Escape the cold weather
- New business opportunities
- Make the pension stretch
- Tired of the rat race
- Get more for their money
- Spiritual renewal
- Tired of high taxes
- Seeking adventure
- Escape from high crime
- Learn a second language

Don't, Kohls advises, succumb to the temptation of criticizing your new country, and stay away from other foreigners who do. Instead, seek out some sympathetic friends. Learn to laugh at frustrating things like government red tape and mile-long bank lines. "To make it in Costa Rica," says one long-time resident, "you need a sense of humor and a good book."

## RESIDENCY REQUIREMENTS

Costa Rica offers several roads to legal residency. You can reside here as a pensioner (pensionado) or a foreigner with a guaranteed income (rentista); an investor; a relative of a resident; or someone with a foreign government assignment on international mission.

Many of Costa Rica's expat's have become permanent or temporary residents in Costa Rica, while others choose to

| \multicolumn{6}{c}{Residency Requirements in Costa Rica} |
|---|---|---|---|---|---|
| **Retired Residents** | **Earning Resident** | **Resident Investor** | **Company Visa** | **Relatives** | **Work Permits** |
| – 600/mo. foreign income. | – $1,000/mo. of local or foreign income (Bank deposit at 5 years expiration) or $60,000 deposit in a Costa Rican savings certificate. | – One-time investment of $50,000-$100,000, $200,000.<br><br>– Cannot exempt vehicle.<br><br>– Cannot exempt household goods. | For export companies having more than 30 full-time employees and a minimum net worth of ¢30 million. For bringing technicians and top executives for up to one year (renewable). | Family ties.<br><br>Marriage | Costa Rican company must initiate |
| – Must stay in country 4 mo. per year (not consecutive). | – Must stay in country 4 mo. per year (not consecutive). | – Must stay in country 6 mo. per year (not consecutive). | | | |
| – Cannot be salaried worker. | – Cannot be salaried worker. | – Can be salaried worker. | – Can earn salary. | | |
| – Can own business and receive income. | – Can own business and receive income. | – Can own business and receive income.<br><br>– Must generate jobs, foreign exchange, technology and benefits to the country which fall within priority segments.<br><br>– Must audit investment each year. | – Cannot exempt vehicle or household goods. | | |
| – Must change the dollars within the National Banking System and keep receipts. | – Must change the dollars within the National Banking System and keep receipts. | | | | |

live in-country by simply renewing their tourist visa as it expires. How you choose to reside depends on your goals and Costa Rican law.

Foreigners, especially U.S. citizens, considering residence abroad often wonder whether the decision will affect their migratory status in their home country. Although many wealthy U.S. citizens voluntarily renounce their native citizenship for the tax benefits of living abroad, accepting a temporary or permanent residence in Costa Rica in no way endangers U.S. citizenship. It will not be necessary to give up your U.S. passport.

The most painless way for the average foreigner to acquire residency is by contacting the Residents Association of Costa Rica at Tel. (506) 233-8068, Fax (506) 222-7862.

The Association has been assisting the newcomer for years, and also offers a variety of practical and social benefits. The following sections will give you an idea about the types of residency status and requirements -- read it before you call.

## *PENSIONADOS AND RENTISTAS*

This used to be the country's most popular residency and retirement program. Until April 1992, the pensioners and foreigners with guaranteed incomes could import their household goods and cars into the country duty-free. But the Costa Rican legislature revoked those tax exemptions as part of a sweeping tax-reform program. Now pensionados and rentistas join the parade of other residents who must pay import taxes of up to 100 percent on the things they bring into the country. As a result, many pensionados and rentistas are looking for other ways to live legally in Costa Rica. And some who were thinking of moving here have changed their minds.

But pensionado-rentista status may still be the quickest and cheapest way to become a temporary resident of Costa Rica. Pensionados must receive at least $600 a month from a qualified pension or retirement plan, or from Social Security.

If your monthly income is less than $600, you may supplement it with a deposit in a Costa Rican bank.

Pensionados may have a bank account here in dollars, but must change at least $600 every month into colones, the national currency, and must live in Costa Rica at least four months a year.

To become a pensionado, according to the Association of Residents of Costa Rica, you need to:

1. Submit your application to the Director of Intelligence and Security (DIS). The form is available at the Costa Rican Tourism Institute (ICT) or the Association of Pensionados and Rentistas. Return it to either office with four photocopies, a certified photocopy of your entire passport and two passport-size photos. These documents are valid for six months. No application will be accepted without DIS approval.

2. Fill out an application for Resident Pensionado or Resident Rentista status. You need to include: full name, nationality, civil status, and occupation; passport number, date, place of issuance and expiration date; names of dependents coming to Costa Rica, civil status, occupation, nationalities, ages, passport numbers, issuance dates, expiration dates and relationship to petitioner; entry date to Costa Rica; statement of willingness to obtain residency as a pensionado or rentista; income origin and amount which satisfies required monthly amount in U.S. dollars; provisional or permanent address in country of origin or in Costa Rica; mailing address. The application must be authenticated by a Costa Rican notary, including legal stamps, duly canceled.

3. Swear before a notary to abide by certain conditions, including agreeing to not engage in remunerated work, inform ICT of any address change, abide by the country's

laws, agree that all privileges derived from the program will benefit only your family, reside in the country at least four months a year and show through government bank receipts the required exchange of dollars to colones for each anniversary year.
4. Submit a certificate showing no police record, issued by a qualified police official nearest to your home. This document is valid for six months from the date it was issued.

5. Go for an INTERPOL check —including fingerprints— in Costa Rica.

6. Submit birth and marriage certificates for yourself and any dependents.

7. Submit a certified photocopy of the entire passport for yourself and any dependents. The copy must have the notation of a public notary or consul of its number, name of bearer, number of pages and notary seal on each page.

8. Submit a certificate issued by the Costa Rican Immigration Council for you and your dependents.

9. Submit 12 passport-size photos, six front view and six profile of yourself and dependents."

As a rentista, you must prove that you have investments outside of the country that will guarantee you at least $1,000 a month for five years. Or you can buy a certificate of deposit from a Costa Rican bank that will guarantee you monthly interest income of $1,000. You must change that $1,000 into colones.

If you deposit $60,000 in a Costa Rican savings certificate in colones for a period of five years, you can also qualify for rentista status. Rentistas must live in the country at least six months a year.

For both pensionados and rentistas, the source of monthly

> **REMEMBER!**
> **The petitioner must provide the following documents from his or her home country:**
>
> 1. **Police certificate of good conduct** It must correspond to your last six months of residency.
> 2. **Birth certificate** That of the petitioner and those of the petitioner's dependents.
> 3. **Marriage certificate** Only if married.
> 4. **Income certificate** Provides proof of income. The wording of this document is very important. Be sure to check with a Costa Rican attorney.
>
> All documents must be authenticated by the Costa Rican consul in your home country. They charge around $50 per document.

income must be certified by company officers. Certified public accountants must verify the companies involved and the source of income. Once everything is verified (and don't be surprised if government officials want it RE-verified), you can start the application process.

Both pensionados and rentistas must renew their identification (called a carnet) every two years. This costs $100. The carnet must be carried at all times. Pensionados and rentistas can set up their own businesses and pay taxes on the money they receive, but they cannot work for someone else unless they obtain a work permit. Pensionados and rentistas pay no taxes on the money they receive from outside Costa Rica.

The application process can take anywhere from a few weeks to a year, but the average time is two to four months. The process requires many documents, including a letter from your police department showing you have no criminal record, birth and marriage certificates and numerous copies of your passport. These documents have to be translated into Spanish and notarized by officials at the Costa Rican consulate nearest you.

Doing the application yourself can be like walking through a jungle without a guide. You'll run into people here who said they did the whole thing themselves and got the status in one or two months, but these are people who have a lot of patience and a fairly good understanding of Spanish. Most people who apply to become pensionados and rentistas either hire a lawyer or go through the residents association. Ask for recommendations before hiring a lawyer. The residents association now charges $700 to process an application. But they speak English and will help you every step of the way.

### *INVESTOR*

This status is called rentista-inversionista. It is granted to people who invest at least $50,000 in special projects like reforestation, tourism and exports, and $100,000 to $200,000 in any other business in Costa Rica. You must reside in Costa Rica at least six months of every year.

### ¡PURA VIDA!

The mutating Tico car: Adapt or risk extinction.

As a rentista-inversionista, you have temporary residency for two years. If there are no problems, you may then become a permanent resident. Requirements include an official application, a $1,000 payment to the Center for Promotion of Exports and Investments (CENPRO), birth and marriage certificates, a police statement, medical tests and passport copies and photos. All must be translated into Spanish by official translators.

You also need to present bank references and a feasibility study if you are starting a project. If you are buying land for the project, you need to submit a copy of the deed of sale and the registration of the land. If your project is tourism, you need a certificate stating so from the Costa Rican Tourism Institute. And if you are investing in an established company, you need to submit the latest balance sheets from this company along with a profit-loss statement. Both need to be certified by an authorized public accountant.

To renew your status, you must present statements of your investments, a profit-loss sheet, a certificate proving payment of taxes and a stock certificate, among other documents.

After two years as a pensioner, rentista or investor, you can apply for permanent residency without the trouble of proving your income every year. After five years as a resident, you may apply for Costa Rican citizenship; it is no longer necessary to renounce your U.S. citizenship to do so.

## *RESIDENT AS A FIRST-DEGREE RELATIVE*

This is probably the quickest way to residency, but it's also somewhat limited unless you have a family in Costa Rica or marry into one. First-degree relatives are parents, siblings, spouses or children. As a resident of a relative, you can do anything in Costa Rica but vote.

To apply you need to submit an official application, birth certificates for you and your family members, a police record, a marriage certificate, passport copies and photos and documentation of your relationship. Relatives of foreigners who become Costa Rican residents are also eligible for residency.

## WORK PERMITS IN COSTA RICA

The government will theoretically issue work permits for certain jobs if employers can prove they can't find qualified Costa Ricans. But pensionados and rentistas need to become permanent residents in order to get a work permit. Permanent residents under the pensionados and rentistas status are not able to work in Costa Rica, although they may create, manage and profit from their own Costa Rican corporation.

For those in-country under other residency statuses, work permits are usually acquired through your employer. If you leave the job, you lose the permit. With a work permit you must pay taxes but you will also receive the same benefits as Costa Ricans, such as Social Security and a mandatory Christmas bonus.

Many pensionados and rentistas opt for volunteer work. There are plenty of volunteer jobs in Costa Rica, including teaching English, advising small businesses, and working in children's hospitals. Or you can start your own business. In that case, you need to read the chapters, Making Money and Small Business Start-ups.

## TOURIST

Canadians, U.S. citizens, and nationals of most European countries can stay in Costa Rica for 90 days without a visa, provided they travel with a passport. Australian, French, Irish and New Zealand citizens are still limited to 30 days.

"Prórrogas de turismo" or extensions of 90-day tourist visas are not available, except for reasons or sickness or other emergencies. Foreigners who are granted only 30-day tourist visas on entry may apply for 30 or 60-day extensions at the Department of Immigration (on the road to the international airport, across from Hospital México). You will need your passport, three photos, a ticket out of the country, and $200 in cash or travelers' checks for each additional month you plan to stay.

If you overstay your 90 days, you will need to report to Immigration to get an exit visa to leave the country. Once Immigration officials stamp your passport, you will have five days to leave the country, failure to do so could result in deportation.

Overstayed tourists are fined ¢320 ($1.50) per month, and are required to pay an exit tax of approximately ¢7,000 ($32) that normally only corresponds to Costa Rican citizens and residents.

If this seems complicated and time consuming, many travel agents will do this entire procedure for you for about $5, even if you have not purchased your ticket from them. Two whole working days are required for processing.

If you want to spend more time in Costa Rica than your 90-day tourist visa allows, the most practical option is to simply leave the country for a quick break in Nicaragua, Panama, or elsewhere, just before your visa expires. You can then return to Costa Rica 72 hours later for another 90-day stint.

### Tips for Success

*WARNING: In the past, it was common among many foreigners to live and do business in Costa Rica as "perpetual tourists." They would simply renew their tourist visas by leaving the country for 72 hours when their visa expired. Many would even stay in the country with an expired visa.*

*Immigration officials are closely watching the frequency that tourists enter, exit and re-enter the country. Tourists found in violation of the country's immigration laws run the risk of being deported and forbidden to re-enter for 10 years.*

*If you own real estate, a business, or just want to feel secure in your adopted country, it is best to obtain legal residency.*

# SCHOOLS & UNIVERSITIES

Education is often the single most important factor for a family living abroad.

The choices are many, but the dilemma is finding an institution that meets the intellectual needs, interests, demands and individual circumstances of your family.

Costa Rica's education system offers quality educational opportunities that often differ from what school-age kids and young people are accustomed to back home. For this reason, many choose private, "international" schools with yearly schedules, teaching philosophies and curriculum similar to the U.S. and Canadian standard.

## WHAT DO INTERNATIONAL SCHOOLS OFFER?

The country's international schools cater to every interest and pocketbook. Classes often meet North American or British standards in teaching methods. They are always bilingual, offering Spanish as a second language to non-native speakers.

They vary in size, from kindergarten through grade 12. Some may offer preparation for international baccalaureate or European Baccalaureate. In the upper grades, the teachers tend to be mainly U.S. citizens preparing students for higher education in the U.S.

Costa Rica prides itself on its educated population and was one of the first countries in Central America to require mandatory schooling for grades one through six. Kindergarten may soon also be a requirement. It's no surprise that the country is full of first-rate public and private schools.

A good selection of English-speaking schools are located in Costa Rica's densely populated Central Valley. Even some rural areas, such as Monteverde, have bilingual classes. Many excellent institutions in the San José suburbs offer first-rate curriculums and the best bilingual teachers in a country-like setting.

Older students will find that Costa Rica has a number of public and private universities. Many have exchange programs with schools in the United States and Europe.

The country's many language schools teach a lot more than Spanish. Students learn Costa Rican culture, cooking, dance and more. These schools are available nation-wide and offer an unmatched primer for anyone wishing to become more familiar with the country.

## EDUCATION IN STATISTICS

| | |
|---|---|
| Mean years of schooling | |
| Male | 5.6 |
| Female | 5.8 |
| Adult literacy (over age 15) | |
| Adults age 15-19 | 97% |
| Male | 93% |
| Female | 93% |
| % enrolled in primary schools | 100% |
| % enrolled in secondary school | 42% |
| % enrolled in university/trade school | 26% |
| Years to produce sixth grade student | 7.5 |
| % of national budget spent on education | 25% |
| Public education expenditure as % of GDP | 4.6% |

*Source: Inside Costa Rica, by Silvia Lara, Tom Barry and Peter Simonson*

## PRIMARY AND SECONDARY SCHOOLS

It's possible to send your child to an all-English school or a bilingual one, where some of the classes are taught in Spanish. Many are accredited in the United States, as well as Costa Rica.

Schools operating on the U.S. schedule start classes in August or September and finish in May or June. Classes on the Costa Rican schedule start in February and run until December.

Tuitions vary greatly. In addition to the yearly fees, the schools listed below also charge for registration and special services such as bus transportation. All the ones listed have excellent reputations.

**Some English-only schools include:**

**The British School.** This school in Santa Catalina, west of San José, has more than 800 students. Its curriculum is based on the United Kingdom system. It has kindergarten through grade 11 on the Costa Rican schedule. Annual tuition runs $1,200 to $2,000. Apdo. 8184-1000, San José. Tel.: 220-0719 or 220-0131.

**Costa Rica Academy.** This school in the western San José suburb of Cariari, has pre-kindergarten through grade 12. It's accredited by the Southern Association of Schools and Colleges in the United States, with a U.S. curriculum. It's on the U.S. schedule. Annual tuition ranges from $1,600 to $4,400. Apdo. 4941-1000, San José. Tel.: (506) 239-0376.

**Country Day School.** Located in the western suburb of Escazú, classes run from pre-kindergarten through grade 12. It's on the U.S. schedule. Annual tuition ranges from $1,500 to $4,620. Apdo. 8-6170-1000, San José. Tel.: (506) 228-0873 or 228-0385. Fax: 289-6789.

**Lincoln School.** Classes are pre-kindergarten through grade 12 at this school in Moravia, northeast of San José. It's accredited by the Southern Association of Schools and Colleges in the United States. It's on the Costa Rican schedule. Annual tuition is $1,000-$2,000 with a one-time family membership fee. Apdo. 1919, San José. Tel.: 235-7733. Fax: 236-1706.

**Marian Baker School.** This school, owned by long-time educator Marian Baker, has a U.S. curriculum for its kindergarten through grade 12 classes. The school is located in San Ramón de Tres Ríos, east of San José. It's on the U.S. schedule. Annual tuition is $3,600 to $4,200. Apdo. 4269-1000, San José. Tel.: (506) 273-3426. Fax: 273-4619.

**Some excellent English and Spanish schools include:**

**Creative Learning Center.** For those who live out in the country -- and we're talking waaayyy out -- this school in Monteverde is a good choice. Classes go from kindergarten through grade four on the Costa Rican schedule. Annual tuition is $350 TO $490. Apdo. 3702-1000, San José. Tel.: (506) 228-5529.

**Methodist School.** This school has its high school (through grade 11) in the eastern suburbs of Sabanilla and its primary school in San Pedro, near the university. It's on the Costa Rican schedule. Rates on request. Apdo. 931-1000, San José. Tel. (506) 225-0655.

**Saint Francis College.** Located in Moravia, northeast of San José, this school has some 1,500 students. Classes are kindergarten through grade 11, on the Costa Rican schedule. Rates on request. Apdo. 4405-1000, San José. Tel.: (506) 235-6685.

**Teocali Academy.** This school in the Guanacaste city of Liberia has classes in Spanish with intensive English courses. Classes are prekindergarten through grade 10. It's on the Costa Rican schedule. Call for updated tuition rates. Apdo. 186-5000, Liberia. Tel: 666-0273.

## *UNIVERSITIES*

Most universities in Costa Rica have entrance requirements similar to those in the United States. Entry into almost all undergraduate programs requires high school transcripts. Most graduate programs require a bachelor's degree. Tuition varies greatly from school to school. Often the price for foreigners is higher than for residents.

Annual tuition costs range from about $2,000 to attend the public University of Costa Rica in San Pedro to $15,000 to get into the graduate program at the Escuela de Agricultura de la Región Tropical Húmeda (EARTH).

**The major public universities of Costa Rica include:**

**University of Costa Rica** (Universidad de Costa Rica). This is the largest university in Costa Rica. Its main campus is in the eastern San José suburb of San Pedro, with branches in Turrialba, Puntarenas, San Ramón, and Limón.

It offers a wide range of degrees, including special programs for foreign students. Sección de Administración, Oficina de Registro, Ciudad Universitaria Rodrigo Facio, San Pedro de Montes de Oca. Tel.: (506) 253-5323. Fax: 234-0452.

**National University** (Universidad Nacional). This is a general university, offering a wide variety of courses and degrees. It is located in Heredia, with regional centers in Liberia, Chorotega, and Pérez Zeledón. Apdo. 86-3000, Heredia. Tel.: (506) 237-6363

**State Correspondence University** (Universidad Estatal a Distancia). This school offers degrees in business administration, education and health. It's based in San Pedro, with campuses in all areas of the country. Apdo. 474-2050, San Pedro de Montes de Oca. Tel.: (506) 253-2121. Fax: 253-4990.

**Technical Institute of Costa Rica** (Instituto Tecnológico de Costa Rica). The Institute offers technical, scientific, and vocational training. Its main campus is in Cartago, with branches in San José and San Carlos. Departamento de Admisión y Registro, Apdo. 159-7050, Cartago. Tel.: (506) 551-5333.

## Some of Costa Rica's top private universities are:

**The Adventist University of Central America** (Universidad Adventista de Centroamérica). This religion-oriented school, based in Alajuela, offers courses in business administration, secretarial skills, elementary education and theology. Apdo. 138, Alajuela. Tel.: (506) 441-5622.

**Autonomous University of Central America** (Universidad Autónoma de Centroamérica). This San José school consists of 12 autonomous liberal arts colleges, modeled after Oxford and Cambridge. Apdo. 7637-1000, San José. Tel.: (506) 234-0701.

**Escuela de Agricultura de la Región Tropical Húmeda (EARTH).** Tropical humid agriculture and conservation of natural resources are among the degrees offered by this institute in the town of Pocora on the Atlantic Coast. Apdo. 4442-1000, Curridabat, San José. Tel.: (506) 253-0240 or 255-2000.

**Universidad Mundial.** This school was once run by Quakers. Now it's affiliated with the Long Island University in Southampton, N.Y. It offers liberal arts courses with an emphasis on hands-on projects and intensive reading. Students must spend their first semester in New York. Friends World Program, Long Island University, Southampton Campus, Southampton, New York 11968. Costa Rica Tel.: (506) 240-7057.

**Interamerican University of Costa Rica** (Universidad Interamericana de Costa Rica). This business school has a general MBA program and a special program for experienced managers. Apdo. 6495-1000, San José. Tel. (506) 225-3745.

**Instituto Centroamericano para la Administración de Empresas, INCAE** (Central American Institute of Business Adminstration). Masters' degrees in business administration, administration of natural resources, and economics are the features of this Alajuela school. Its MBA program is modeled after the Harvard Business School. Apdo. 960-4050, Alajuela. Tel. (506) 443-0506.

**University for Peace** (Universidad para la Paz). You'll find changing courses and graduate degree programs at this university in Ciudad Colón. Concentrations include: ecology, communications, human rights, and social integration. Apdo. 138, Ciudad Colón. Tel.: (506) 249-1511. Fax: 249-1929.

## SPANISH SCHOOLS

If you are a foreigner coming to Costa Rica to study the language, you will find plenty of schools offering intensive Spanish courses. Many offer a variety of programs including homestays that enable students to live with Costa Rican families, as well as offer cooking classes, dance classes, field trips and tours.

If you want to explore Costa Rica before moving here, these schools offer excellent opportunities to pick up a basic knowledge of the language while you get to know the country.

**Costa Rica Spanish Institute (COSI).** This institute offers Spanish for specific purposes: business, medicine, education, social sciences, computers, etc. in a relaxed atmosphere. It's located in Zapote, a residential suburb of San José. Apdo. 1366-2050 San Pedro, San José, Costa Rica, Tel/Fax: (506) 253-2117.

**Centro Lingüístico Conversa (CONVERSA).** Established in 1975, Conversa offers intensive Spanish programs on its six-acre mountainside campus in Santa Ana, which includes outdoor classrooms, recreation facilities, two lodges and swimming pool. Homestay or on-campus lodging options. Apdo 17-1007 Centro Colón. Tel. (506) 221-7649 or toll-free 1-800-354-5036 from U.S.A. and Canada.

**Instituto Británico.** This school has classrooms in San José and in Liberia, in the Guanacaste province. It offers language classes alone or in conjunction with a culture program that includes lectures and lodging with a Costa Rican family. Apdo. 8184-1000, San José. Tel.: (506) 234-9054 or 225-0256.

**Latin American Institute of Language (ILISA).** You can choose from several levels of language courses, a history and culture program, and private tutoring at this San Pedro school. Prices on request. Apdo. 1001-2050, San Pedro. Tel.: (506) 225-2495, 225-5413, or call toll-free from the United States or Canada: 1-800-Espanol.

### Tips for Success

*Thoroughly research all available options before choosing a school for your children. Costa Rica has many good private schools, but each has its own style and atmosphere.*

*To enjoy the bicultural experience to the fullest, we recommend choosing a school with a good Spanish as a second language program.*

*But kids aren't the only ones who need to consider education. We recommend that parents also take a full-immersion Spanish course to get the most out of their new Costa Rican experience.*

# MOVING YOUR FURNITURE

Moving across town, let alone to another country, is hardly an easy task. It requires a lot of decisions — what to take, what to leave, what to throw away, what to live without.

People planning to move to Costa Rica should prepare themselves for a lot of organizing, a lot of waiting and a lot of expenses. The Costa Rican government taxes many imported goods — even used imported goods.

For instance, records and compact discs are taxed at 42 percent of their value. Refrigerators and stoves are taxed at 60 percent. Bedding and towels are taxed at 99 percent. And the Costa Rican customs agents decide what the value of each object is. Two shipments, exactly the same, could have completely different tax amounts, depending on the customs agents who examine them.

So you won't know until you get here how much you'll have to pay. The general manager of the Residents' Association of Costa Rica, estimates an average tax charge of $6,000 to $7,000, if you move your entire three-bedroom house. But it can easily go higher if you're bringing in a lot of things.

You will also be taxed on your shipping costs. Costa Rican moving experts recommend shipping your things domestically to a city close to Costa Rica, like New Orleans or Miami. That way the government can tax you only on shipping charged from that city to Costa Rica. This can mean a considerable tax savings, especially if you're moving from someplace like Vancouver, B.C.

People coming from Europe should check to find which city offers the least expensive passage to Costa Rica and ship from there.

Check the prices of a number of international moving companies in the city you decide to ship from, just as you would if you were moving within your country. Shippers will get your things as far as Costa Rican customs. It's up to you and the Costa Rican government to negotiate from there.

To reduce shipping and tax expenses, go through your belongings very carefully. Try to get rid of anything bulky. Some of the best things to leave behind are large household appliances like refrigerators and stoves. A new refrigerator might cost more in Costa Rica than in the United States, but by the time you pay shipping costs AND taxes on your old one it will probably be worth it to buy the refrigerator here.

Furniture, especially wooden furniture, is cheap and easy to buy in Costa Rica. Dad's old rocking chair is better left behind. Even if customs agents decide the chair itself is worthless, you'll still have to pay taxes on shipping costs.

Carry as much as you can on the plane, especially small, valuable items like jewelry or silverware. Used, personal things are not taxed at the airport. You should also bring with you everything you think you'll need to live for a few months -- the items you ship could get held up in customs for as little as a few days or as long as several months.

You can ship your belongings in large containers or in small boxes. What you do will depend on what you have and what you plan to ship. If you opt for the big containers, make sure you fill them up, but be careful about packing clothes in with your other things. Used clothing and books are not taxed. Packed in separate boxes, they should clear customs fairly quickly. But if you mix them with, say, towels and bedding, which are taxed at 99 percent of their estimated value, you could be going a long time without your favorite outfit.

Label your containers carefully and make lists of everything you are taking, as well as its estimated value. These will help move your things through customs more quickly.

For expert advice and shipping services you can contact Latti Express Co. in Miami (305) 593-8929, Fax (305) 593-8786 or San José, Costa Rica (506) 296-0806, Fax (506) 231-7957. Or call the "Transfer Car Department" at the moving company, Mudanzas Mundiales S.A., Tel: (506) 253-6464, Fax: (506) 253-3389. In Costa Rica call them at 800-664-6464. Both these companies are experts.

*Even shipping agents will tell you that it is better to buy your household appliances and furnishings in Costa Rica than go to the trouble and expense of shipping everything down.*

*Although the country's high import duties on these durable goods translate into higher prices to the consumer, the government has established a "duty free zone" in the south Pacific port of Golfito where these items can be purchased economically.*

*At the port of Golfito you can buy everything from electronics and major appliances, to clothing and even imported liquor. Costa Ricans make the pilgrimage regularly.*

*Furniture can be purchased new in San José. Sometimes prices are lower in small Central Valley towns. Many furniture makers will economically custom-build wood furniture to your specifications. Good deals are also available on used furniture -- check The Tico Times weekly classified ads.*

# BRINGING YOUR CAR

Cars are expensive in Costa Rica, and poor road conditions age them rapidly. Most are Japanese, but their standards and quality are not the same as those manufactured to be sold in the United States. Nevertheless, even old beaters are priced as if they were in great condition.

Spare parts for cars bought in the U.S. are not easily available here, although the market for them is growing, and courier services can bring them in quite rapidly.

If you decide to bring your car with you, the procedure begins with shipping. Shipping time by boat is about a week from Miami to the Atlantic port of Limón. Three more days are required to get the car through customs. Shipping charges are around $800 to $900 from Miami and $1,200 from California or New York, plus an additional $100 to $150 for documentation and customs inspection at exit port.

You can also send it by plane at a cost of about $1,500, but space is not readily available for cars on cargo airlines that cover the Miami-Costa Rica route. Florida West, Challenge, Arrow and LACSA are among the possible airlines for this service.

Once your car arrives, complicated customs procedures all but mandate the services of a customs broker.

At the port of arrival you pay the corresponding taxes, which are established at 101 percent of the value assessed by the customs agent for an automobile -- or only 74 percent for pickups -- plus the value of shipping charges and insurance. The assessed value is the manufacturer's suggested retail price when the car was new, as determined by the customs official.

Duties are discounted depending on the age of the vehicle. One-year-old cars are not entitled to discount; however, two-year-old vehicles receive a 10 percent discount, three-year-olds receive a 20 percent discount, four-year-olds a 50 percent discount, and vehicles five years or older will be discounted 70 percent.

### How to Figure Taxes on a Five-year-old Vehicle

| | |
|---|---|
| *Vehicle's assessed value : | $10,000 |
| Less 70% discount on assessed price: | $3,000 |
| Plus shipping: | $800 |
| Plus insurance: | $87 |
| Total taxable: | $3,887 |

**Now, to calculate the import duty, take:**

| | |
|---|---|
| The total taxable (above) | $3,887 |
| Plus 101% tax (1.01 x $3,887) | $3,926 |
| **Total Taxes Due:** | **$3,926** |

These rates are constantly changing. Use figures above as a rule-of-thumb.

*Manufacturer's suggested retail determined by customs official.

Now that your car has been authorized to enter the country, next comes the process of registration, which will take about ten days. This involves taking the car to the Ministry of Public Works and Transportation (MOPT) for a check up. With the document issued there you are authorized to nationalize the vehicle, which is done at the Public Registry. Payment at the Registry will be approximately $300, depending on the make of the car and its assessed value. Once the Registry issues the proper documents, you return to the Ministry of Public Works and Transportation, where your license plates will be issued years later.

All the preceding involves long lines, waiting and extreme patience, but if you get advice from an expert with good contacts, your part in the whole procedure will be limited to signing final papers. Never entrust money or important documents to anyone who doesn't come highly recommended.

If you bring a car as a tourist, your passport will be stamped with a three-month vehicle permit visa, which can be extended to six months. But beware! In the past, the three-month extension was automatic. Now it must be approved by the Ministry of Transport (MOPT). To date, all the extensions have been approved. At the end of the six-month period, you either leave the country with your car or pay the corresponding taxes to keep it here.

If you decide to remain in Costa Rica beyond the six-month grace period, but don't wish to pay import duties and taxes on your vehicle, it will be impounded by the customs office until payment is received, or the vehicle is sold.

If the vehicle stamp in your passport is still valid when the six-month car visa expires, you will not be permitted to leave the country until you sell the vehicle, pay the necessary taxes or place the vehicle in customs. If you insist on a do-it-yourself, you can obtain general information from:

Dirección General de Aduanas (Customs), tel: (506) 256-3011.

Ministerio de Obras Públicas y Transportes, MOPT (Ministry of Public Works and Transport) (506) 257-7798, Ext. 512 or 550, Plaza Víquez.

Registro Público (Public Registry) (506) 224-0628 or 258-8115, Registro de Vehículos (Vehicle Section), Zapote.

For expert advice and shipping services you can contact Latti Express Co. in Miami (305) 593-8929, Fax (305) 593-8786 or San José, Costa Rica (506) 296-0806, Fax (506) 231-7957. Or call the "Transfer Car Department" at the moving company, Mudanzas Mundiales S.A., Tel: (506) 253-6464,

Fax: (506) 253-3389. In Costa Rica call them at 800-664-6464. Both these companies are experts.

 **Tips for Success**

*Your customs agent in Costa Rica can calculate your vehicle's duties and taxes even before it leaves its country of origin. Simply forward to the agent a copy of the vehicle's title, including identification number, year, model, make and body style. Agencies usually charge a small fee for this service.*

*Before you ship the car, be sure to remove anything that could be easily stolen, such as the radio, tools, spare parts etc. We've even heard of license plates and rear view mirrors that were stolen by customs officials or dock workers with sticky fingers.*

**¡PURA VIDA!**

*Crater-like potholes are common on Costa Rica's roads.*

# AUTO INSURANCE

All insurance in Costa Rica -- including auto -- is sold exclusively by the National Insurance Institute (INS). Auto insurance applies to the vehicle, regardless of who is driving, and covers as long as the driver has a locally issued, valid Costa Rican drivers license. A drivers license from abroad is acceptable if the driver acquires a vehicle stamp from customs (see the previous chapter), and is 18 or older.

Cars with foreign license plates will be issued coverage only for **personal liability** and **property damage to third parties** and only for the exact period of time governed by the temporary vehicle stamp in the owner's passport -- usually 90 days. This can be extended for an additional 90 days with the renewal of the tourist visa. This type of policy is good only in Costa Rica.

This no-fault coverage is mandatory for all foreign-plated cars. It costs about $50.00 for each three-month period, plus a $25.00 to $75.00 road tax, depending on the type of car. A car with foreign plates may be legally driven only by its registered owner.

**There are two types of auto insurance:**

**Obligatory**: Carried by all motor vehicles circulating in the country, it is renewed automatically every year along with the license tags, for $25 to $35 per year. It covers injury to anyone in an accident involving the insured vehicle. Its limits are approximately $3,400 per accident.

**Supplementary:** Covers personal liability in excess of limits of the obligatory policy. This is optional, so nobody has the authority to request to see your policy.

To apply for this insurance, contact an INS agent, such as Dave or Mike Garrett at Garrett and Associates, Tel. (506) 233-2455. The following information will also come in handy:

**The coverage options available include:**

**Personal Liability:** Covers personal liability established by the courts as a result of death or injury caused by an accident for which the driver of your vehicle was held responsible. Does not cover injury or death of family members or employees of the insured party or driver.

**Property Damage:** Covers damage caused by your vehicle to property (car, house, etc.) belonging to third parties, if the accident was the fault of the driver of your vehicle.

**Collision:** Covers damage sustained by your vehicle due to a collision with another vehicle, whether the accident was the fault of the person driving your car, or when the person driving the other car has no insurance or cannot pay.

**Fire:** Covers damage to your vehicle caused by fire, either by internal or external factors.

**Theft:** Covers loss of the vehicle. If the vehicle is recovered, the policy pays for damage or missing parts. If not recovered, the entire insured amount is paid or the vehicle replaced. Items left in the vehicle are not covered.

**Combination of Additional Risks:** Covers damage resulting from floods, hurricanes, cyclones, earthquakes, external explosions, vandalism, strikes, riots, falling objects, partial theft, crashing against inanimate objects etc. Within certain rules, you can select the coverages that you need: you pay for what you get.

Auto insurance policies are normally issued for six months; after expiring you have a two-week grace period to renew.

The annual premium varies according to the fair market price of the vehicle, but it is approximately $850 per $10,000. The higher the insured value, the higher the premium. It is advisable not to overvalue your car, because if the vehicle is stolen or totaled in an accident, INS has the option to either pay you the insured value or buy you another similar car. If your car is overinsured, INS will logically replace it, rather than pay.

Since car insurance in Costa Rica is in the name of the vehicle owner and not the driver, a person's driving record has no direct influence on the cost of the policy. A system of surcharges and bonus discounts on insurance premiums is in place that rewards those who file few claims.

Specifically, if the INS pays a claim, whether or not the policy holder or driver was at fault in the accident, the premium will be raised. The percentage of increase (we've seen as high as 100 percent!) is calculated by the INS based on the amount of the claim paid in relation to the premiums received. If a policy has no claims against it in two years, premium bonuses are applied. They start at 5 percent and increase every year.

## ¡PURA VIDA!

Traveling the highways, beware of slow moving ox carts.

## AUTO ACCIDENTS

Follow these steps if you are involved in an accident:
1. **Location**   Make sure you know where you are and can give directions "Tico style" (See Numbering of Streets).
2. **Severe Injuries**   Call a "Cruz Roja" ambulance at 128 or 911.
3. **Call the Cops**   Call a traffic cop, called a *tráfico* (222-9245 or 222-9330) who will go to the scene of the accident. He will give each driver a green ticket or citation to appear at the traffic court in the nearest *alcaldía* or city hall. Ask him where and when you should go. If you fail to appear on the scheduled date you could be found guilty by default.
4. **Call the National Insurance Institute (INS)**   Call 800-800-8000 and ask them to send an adjuster. Give your policy number. Take the name of the INS operator, particularly if you are told the INS adjuster can't go. The adjuster will fill out an accident report and give you further instructions.
5. **Take Names and Addresses**   Jot down the phone numbers and other details of witnesses, as well as of the other car and driver.
6. **Drinking**   If you think the other driver has been drinking, ask the cop to give him a breathalyzer test, called an *alcoholemia*. Also point this out to the INS adjuster.
7. **Do Not Assume Any Obligations or Responsibility** or make a "deal" with the other parties involved in the accident.

### Tips for Success

*Many Costa Ricans and foreign residents register their vehicle in the name of their Costa Rican corporation. That way if the vehicle is involved in an accident and sued, the corporation is liable for the damages and not the owner personally (see chapter on Offshore Corporations).*

# OBTAINING A DRIVERS LICENSE

Foreigners don't qualify for a Costa Rican driver's license unless they are residents of the country. Anyone with approved temporary residency, such as a student visa, can get a Costa Rican license with proof of their legal status. The following tips will help residents and temporary residents obtain a drivers license:

Go to the Dirección de Transporte Automotor in San José at Avenida 18 and Calle 5 (telephones 527-2188 and 223-4626). There are several young men working at the entrance who will direct you, free-of-charge. They may offer to help you with the entire process, for a fee, but beware, because scamsters abound. You must have with you: a valid passport, an original current driver's license from your country, and a copy of your current driver's license.

You will be directed to an office nearby where you obtain your "medical certificate." This consists of an eye exam and answering some health questions at a cost of about ₡1,200. The medical examiner will sign the certificate, which you must take, along with the other items mentioned above, back to the Oficina de Transporte. If your current driver's license has expired, you must also take a written examination.

You will then be directed to the appropriate lines to deliver documents and have your picture taken. To avoid long lines, it's best to arrive when the office first opens at 8 a.m. The cost of the license averages $16.00, and it's valid for three years.

# COSTA RICAN
## CONSULATES & EMBASSIES

It is necessary to have certain documents notarized by a Costa Rican Consulate or Embassy when obtaining residency or when taking care of other official business. The following lists some of the consulates and embassies abroad.

### UNITED STATES

**Arizona**
Phoenix
Tel:    (602) 231-3689
Fax:   (602) 231-2388

**California**
Los Angeles
Tel:    (213) 380-6031
          (213) 380-7915
Fax:   (213) 380-5639

San Diego
Tel/Fax: (619) 571-6875

San Francisco
Tel/Fax: (415) 392-3745

**Colorado**
Denver
Tel:    (303) 696-8211
Fax:   (303) 696-1110

**Florida**
Tampa
Tel:    (813) 726-1929
Fax:   (813) 726-1807

Miami
Tel:    (305) 871-7485
          (305) 871-8487
Fax:   (305) 871-0860

**Georgia**
Atlanta
Tel:    (404) 951-7025
Fax:   (404) 951-7073

**Illinois**
Chicago
Tel:    (312) 263-2772
Fax:   (312) 263-5807

## Massachusetts
Boston
Tel: (617) 738-9709

Springfield
Tel: (413) 781-5400
Fax: (413) 739-0801

## Lousiana
New Orleans
Tel: (504) 887-8131
Fax: (504) 887-0916

## Minnesota
St. Paul
Tel: (612) 481-3618
Fax: (612) 645-4684

## New York
New York City
Tel: (212) 425-2620
     (212) 425-2621
Fax: (212) 785-6818

## Texas
Houston
Tel: (713) 266-0484
Fax: (713) 266-1527

San Antonio
Tel: (210) 699-6515
Fax: (210) 824-8489

## Washington D.C.

Embassy
Tel: (202) 234-2945
    (202) 234-2946
    (202) 234-8653

Consulate
Tel: (202) 328-6628
Fax: (202) 265-4795

## CANADA

### Montréal, Québec
Tel: (514) 393-1057
Fax: (514) 393-1624

### Vancouver, B.C.
Tel/Fax: (604) 681-2152

### Toronto, Ontario
Tel: (416) 961-6773
Fax: (416) 961-6771

### Saskatoon, Sask.
Tel: (306) 934-5003
Fax: (306) 975-1187

# CLUBS & GROUPS

**H**ere's a list that will make you feel at home. Check The Tico Times newspaper for the most recent contacts and phone numbers.

| | | |
|---|---|---|
| **12-STEP GROUP MEETINGS** | 228-6051 | Overeaters Anonymous, Co-dependents Anonymous. Call for days and times. Unity, 600 meters north of Tega, Escazú |
| **AA MEETINGS IN ENGLISH** | 222-1880 San José, The Gringo-Tico Group. golfito, Pura Vida Group, Puntarenas, 663-0170 | 12-step programs. Check days and times. |
| **AMERICAN LEGION POST 10** | 228-1740, after 2 p.m. | Escazú |
| **AMERICAN LEGION POST 11** | Commander Bill Clifford 221-9320 | Meets second Saturday of the month at the Amstel Hotel, Parque Morazán. |
| **AMERICAN LEGION POST 16** | Ken Brown, 450-0407 | Heredia |
| **AMERICAN LEGION POST 12** | Commander Ron Kalman 775-0409 | Golfito |
| **AMERICAN LEGION POST 15** | Apdo. 90, Santa Cruz, Guanacaste | Sugar Beach |
| **AMERICAN POKER CLUB** | 223-4331 | Meets Tuesdays, Thursdays, Saturdays and Sundays. |
| **ANCHOR CLUB OF COSTA RICA** | 222-1880 | Alcoholics Anonymous, Narcotics Anonymous, Codependents Anonymous. Daily meetings. The coffee pot is always on. Call for times. Second floor of Edificio Maryland, Ave. 6, Calle 1, next to "The Candy Shop"-- or from Cine Rex, 100 meters south and 100 meters east. |
| **ASOCIACION NACIONAL DE BRIDGE** | Amalia, 232-9254 John, 253-2762 | Organizes duplicate bridge games and takes part in international contests. Bridge players, novices welcome. Call for partners/hours. |
| **CANADIAN CLUB** | 232-9289 evenings | Holds luncheons every third Wednesday in Hotel Vista de Golf at noon. |

| | | |
|---|---|---|
| CANADIAN CLUB OF COSTA RICA ASSOCIATION | 289-6089 | Don McColl, president, invites all Canadian visitors and residents to attend monthly get-togethers. |
| CHRISTIAN WOMEN'S CLUB | Fran Pannabaker, June MacAdam, 224-9457, Apdo. 6491-1000 San José | Breakfasts every other month with inspirational speakers, welcomes all English-speaking women. |
| CLUB AMATEUR DE PESCA | 232-3430 mornings, Apdo. 3505-3000, San José | Brings anglers of all nationalities together and helps obtain fishing licenses for int'l tournaments, organizes national competitions. |
| CLUB DE JARDINES DE COSTA RICA | 222-0384, Apdo. 5136-1000 San José | Welcomes everyone interested in gardens and plants. Monthly meetings, exhibits, lectures and courses. |
| DEMOCRATS ABROAD | Josephine Stuart, 223-3896 Haegele, 231-5584 | Register U.S. voters, help in absentee balloting, hosts interesting speakers. |
| DISABLED AMERICAN VETERANS | 443-2508, U.S. Embassy, Apdo 920-1200 San José | Meet the first Wednesday of each month at 1:30 p.m. at the Corobicí Hotel. |
| ENGLISH-SPEAKING KIWANIS CLUB | Jerry, 438-0038 Claudio, 224-4320 | Meets first and third Thursday, 12:15 p.m., 5th floor of Gran Hotel for lunch. |
| FREE UNIVERSITY OF COSTA RICA | 232-5539, 250-1553 | English and Spanish conversation programs. No fees/book purchases. |
| HASH HOUSE HARRIERS | Donald Couture, 224-8340 Hash Hotline, 222-3043 | Club of joggers and beer drinkers. Join, jog in San José and meet new people. |
| INVESTMENT CLUB OF COSTA RICA | 240-2240, 232-5539 | Meets monthly at Hotel Le Bergerac. |
| LITTLE THEATER GROUP | John Donahue, 282-7775 Rick Lane, 273-4712 | The country's oldest, presents at least two productions each year, with English-speaking actors. All interested in acting, singing, dancing, directing etc. welcome. |
| NEWCOMERS' CLUB | Lucinda Pyne, 249-1154, 228-6347 | Organizes get-togethers of English-speaking women, features interesting speakers and shares interests or skills. |
| PERSONAL COMPUTER CLUB | 249-1806, 228-0915 | Bilingual, open to anyone who uses IBM compatible personal computer, is over 18, or approved by board of directors. |
| REPUBLICANS ABROAD | Hank Laskey, 273-4276, Louis Larson, 228-0433, Apdo. 1503-1250 Escazú | Sponsor interesting speakers at their luncheon meetings and register U.S. voters. |
| ROTARY CLUB MEETINGS | Alajuela | Mondays, 8 p.m. in club Internacional, 441-2381. |
| | San José | Mondays, 8 p.m., Asociación Gerontológica, 221-0310 |
| | Escazú | Tuesdays, 8 p.m., Apartotel María Alexandra, 228-1507 |

| | | |
|---|---|---|
| **ROTARY CLUB MEETINGS CONT'D** | Puntarenas | Noon, Rotary House, 661-0839 |
| | Nicoya | 8 p.m., Hlth Mnstry Bldg. 685-5021 |
| | San Ramón | 8 p.m., Edif. Municipal, 445-5155 |
| | Rohrmoser | Wednesday, 7:30 p.m., Corobicí Hotel, 232-8122 |
| **SINGLES DANCE** | 228-0900 269-9832 | Sundays, 3-7 p.m. in the Hotel Forest, Escazú, 800 meters east of old Intex factory. |
| **SPANISH/ENGLISH CLUB** | | Wednesdays, 6 p.m. in Librería Heredia. No tuition or fees. You'll be paired with a Tico or Gringo at your conversation level. |

# *SUGGESTED READING*

For additional information on living, visiting or investing in Costa Rica, we've found the following to be most helpful:

**The New Key to Costa Rica**, by Beatrice Blake. Ulysses Press, Berkeley, California. A well-organized guide that provides ample information for both tourist and resident. It is well recommended for anybody visiting Costa Rica.

**Inside Costa Rica**, by Silvia Lara. Resource Center Press, Albuquerque, New Mexico. An excellent and concise look at Costa Rica's politics, economy, society and environment.

**Choose Costa Rica**, by John Howells, Gateway Books, San Rafael, CA. Good general overview about living in the country.

**Purchasing Real Estate in Costa Rica**, by Attorney Alvaro Carballo. Apartado 6997-1000 San José, Costa Rica. Fax: (506) 223-9151. An excellent guide that helps explain the process of purchasing real estate in Costa Rica.

**Driving the Panamerican Highway to Mexico and Central America**, by Raymond & Audrey Pritchard. Costa Rica Books. PO Box 1512 Thousand Oaks, CA 91358. To date the only book on hand that describes a "how to" drive from the U.S. to Central America.

**The Rules of The Game, Buying Real Estate in Costa Rica**, by Bill Baker, 104 Half Moon Circle H-3 Hupoluzo, FL 33462. Excellent advice on how to invest in real estate.

*Continued on next page*

**Insight Guide to Costa Rica**, by Harvey Haber, distributed by Houghton Miflim and Prentice-Hall. A wonderful guide with beautiful colored photos. Enjoyable reading even if you never leave your house.

## PERIODICALS

**The Tico Times Newspaper**, published weekly, Tel: (506) 222-8952, Fax: (506) 233-6378. This paper is your best single source for news about politics, government, the environment, health, police and courts, life and living in Costa Rica. It's "What's Doing" section helps residents all over the country meet new friends and plan their week. Give them a call for yearly subscriptions in Costa Rica and abroad.

**Costa Rica Today Newspaper**, published weekly. Tel: (506) 296-3911, Fax: (506) 232-5693. A nice newspaper for tourists, with plenty of pictures and articles to keep you updated on the latest parades and festivals.

# EMERGENCY PHONE NUMBERS

| | |
|---|---|
| **ALL EMERGENCIES** | **911** |
| Police Department | 117 |
| Fire Department | 118 |

(All of the above only in the Metropolitan Area)

| | |
|---|---|
| San Juan de Dios Hospital (public) | 222-0166 |
| Hospital México (public) | 232-6122 |
| Red Cross Ambulance | 221-5818 |
| U.S. Embassy (8:00 a.m.-4:30 p.m. M-F) | 220-3939 |
| U.S. Embassy (after hours and weekends) | 220-3127 |
| Canadian Embassy | 255-3522 |
| British Embassy | 221-5566 |
| American Express (for loss or theft) | 233-0044 |
| | 223-0116 |
| Visa International | 257-1357 |
| Mastercard | 253-2155 |
| Western Union | 227-7200 |
| Airport Information (24 hours) | 441-0744 |
| Better Business Bureau | 257-5978 |
| Taxi Service | 254-5847 |
| | 235-9666 |
| Local Information | 113 |
| Long Distance Information | 124 |
| Long Distance Operator | 116 |

# SOURCES USED IN COMPILING THIS BOOK

Caribbean Basin 1996
Commercial Profile
Grand Cayman


The Rules of the Game
Bill Baker 1996


The Legal Guide to Costa Rica 1995
Roger Peterson


Purchasing Real Estate in Costa Rica
Alvaro Carballo


U.S. Latin Trade Magazine
Various issues, Jan. - Sept. 1996

# Classified Advertisers

*The following are paid advertisements.
Before choosing the provider of any service in Costa Rica, OG Books highly recommends that our readers research all available possibilities. These companies are a good place to start.*

# FREE RESIDENCY

4 Wks. yearly free lodging with purchase of Government Approved 2.4 acre Site

## $50,000

Includes
All Titles and Deeds
750 acre Forest Reserve
Spectacular 360° Views

### *Earth Council Support*
Costa Rica Immigration approval

Invest • Protect • Preserve

For complete details contact
***MAGIL FOREST LODGE***

San José: Tel: (506)233-5991 / (506)221-2825
Fax: (506)233-3713
P.O. Box 3404 - 1000, Costa Rica

# YOUR MAIL AND PACKAGES ARE IN THE BEST HANDS

## STAR BOX

Star Box offers you a P.O.Box and Physical address in the U.S.A. This service allows you to receive all the benefits that the U.S.A. Postal Service offers.

## EXPRESS SERVICE FOR HEAVY CARGO (MIAMI/ SAN JOSE)

Express delivery for merchandise weighing 100 Lb. or more, we can also consolidate merchandise if desired, our prices are extremely competive. You can combine both services or join only one.

*So call us today!*

Tel:(506)257-3443 - 221-2186 Fax:(506)223-5624

# Professional Service System S.A.  Dental Team

## Advanced Technology At your Service

This dental office provides all the necessary dental procedures to solve your problems based on

**FUNCTION + AESTHETICS = PERSONAL SATISFACTION**

### Dr. Mario Garita, D.D.S.
Director of Center for Dental Implants of Costa Rica
Specialist in Implant Dentistry
University of Miami

### Dr. José R. Garita, D.D.S., M.A.
Director of Professional Service System S.A.
General Practitioner
M.A. at University of Iowa

### Dra. Priscilla M. Rojas, D.D.S.
General Practitioner

*For more information please contact us and we can arrange for your transportation from the airport or hotel.*

**Phone/Fax: (506) 290-1750 / 231-4014**
USA Address: Interlink 329 P.O.Box 02-5635 Miami, Florida 33102
P.O.Box: 333-1200. San José, Costa Rica

# Latti Express Co.
International Transportation Services

## To and from Costa Rica...

Air Freight
Ocean Freight
Machinery & Car Shipping
Household Moves
Customs Brokerage
Purchasing Service -- USA

## Offices in Costa Rica, USA and Canada
-- since 1987 --

**Miami:** Phone: (305) 593-8929
Fax: (305) 593-8786

**San Jose:** Phone: (506) 296-0806
Fax: (506) 231-7957

# Dental Clinic

**Clínica de Restaurativa y Estética Dental**

## Dr. Luis Kaver Fastag

### Restorative & Cosmetic Dentistry

**Baylor College of Dentistry, TEXAS**

### English Spoken

Member of the American Academy of Cosmetic Dentistry

From McDonald's,
La Sabana 100 m. South
P.O. Box 292-1007 San José

**Tel:(506)290-2323**
**Tel / Fax:(506) 290-0303**

*Whoever told you paradise didn't exist?*

We've regained paradise just for you and what's best, added some fun to it. Your piece of paradise includes secluded villas and rooms amidst lush seaside cliffs, two fresh water pools, a tennis court, water sports, deep-sea fishing, diving, adventure tours of the area and more. Now THIS is paradise.

*Sol Playa Hermosa*

# Beach Villas For Sale

Professional Managemet • Rental Income
• Located on the Gold Coast •
• Full Time Maintenance • Security

**Ask about our investor tour specials**

San José Office:　　Sol Playa Hermosa Beach Office:
(506)290-0561　　　　　(506) 670-0345

# Clínica Veterinaria
## Dr Adrián Molina

E S C A Z U

1. Small species & equine clinic.
2. General Surgery
3. X -Rays
4. Import / Export Documentation
5. Vaccinations & deworming programs
6. House Calls
7. Teeth Cleaning
8. Grooming
9. Pet Hotel
10. Training School
11. Pet Shop

ENGLISH SPOKEN

Address: 150 mts. East and 25 South
from Saretto Super Market
P.O.Box 1301-1250 Escazú

**Tels:228-1909 / Emergencies 225-2500
Fax:289-9989**

# Exceptional Investment Opportunities

**PLANET EARTH VISITOR CENTER**

## Planet Earth Visitor Center

### and the Service Support Center

Located at Playa Blanca,
Nicoya Península, Costa Rica

## Be part of the future...

The initial share price only **$35.00**
Exceptional returns benefits

Adventure • Entertainment •
Exhibits to thrill • Educate, amaze and
stimulate the imagination

Contact **NEMUCA S.A.**

Tel:(506)256-0475, (506)257-9661
Tel/Fax:(506) 257-6272

Galería AA, oficina 17 Calle central, ave. 6 y 7 San José
Apdo: 1276 Alajuela, Costa Rica./ SJO 65, Box 025216.Miami FL33102 USA
Email:rpilon@ami.qc.ca/ • http://www.multicr.com/eng/nemuca/

## *Lic. Ronald Blair Houston*

Abogado • Notario
Attorney at Law

## Announcing
## our new office location

*Calle 36,*
*Avenidas. 7 y 9*
*San José, Costa Rica*

**Bufete Houston & Asoc.**

Tel:255-0831 - Telefax:221-3594

P.O.Box:927 Centro Colón
San José, Costa Rica

# Especialidades Odontológicas
# Escazú S.A.

- Surgery and implants
- Endodontics
- Orthodontics
- Periodontics
- Prosthodontics

Dr. José A. Jalet M    Dra. Lorena León B.
Dr. Rolando Guzmán C.   Dr. Esteban Bolaños L.
Dr. Abelardo Gómez

**Centro Comercial
La Rambla, Local # 15
San Rafael de Escazú**

**Tel:228-1456 - Fax:289-9557**

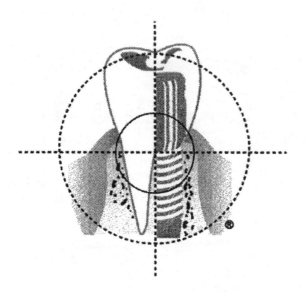

**Dr. Esteban Bolaños Lund, D.D.S., M.Sc.D.**
# Periodontist
**University Hospital of Wales, U.K.**

Diplomate- the American Society
of Osseontegration
International Member -
The American Academy of Periodontology
International Member -
The Academy of Osseointegration

Phone Office #(506) 297-1898 Fax # (506) 236-1884
E-mail: [ebolanos@sol.racsa.co.cr]
P.O.Box # 114-6151, Santa Ana 2000
COSTA RICA

# Rancho Playa Negra
### Guanacaste • Costa Rica

## Best Prices on the Coast

### Private Ocean Front Community
### Lots From $10,000 to $55,000

- Exclusive gated community with 24 hour guard service
- Playa Negra has one of the best and most consistent surf breaks in Costa Rica
- Spectacular views up and down the Pacific Coast. White sand beaches
- Improved building lots from 6,725 sq.ft (river side) to 16,140 sq. (beach side)

For more information contact:Tel:(506)255-1001, Fax:(506)223-6048
Apartado Postal:11557-1000, Costa Rica, Central America
Home page:http://www.anacapa.co.cr

---

## Telegroup Global Access SM

**Who is Telegroup?**
Telegroup Inc. is one of America's largest wholesale buying groups for long distance. Telegroup Global Access now offers the lowest international rates in the world.

**What is Telegroup Global Access?**
Telegroup Global Access is an international service that can save 20% to 55% on intercontinental calls. In the United States it is an "add on" service, which means it can simply be added to whatever long distance service your company is now using.
For locations outside the U.S., we offer Global Access Callback abd Global Access 800 services. Global Access Callback allows overseas customers to bypass the expensive rates charged by most foreign telephone companies and make intercontinental calls at our low U.S.rates. Global Access 800 gives overseas companies an 800 number that can be used by employees and customers in the U.S.

**Benefits of Telegroup Global Access**
**In the United States:**
- Saving up to 50% when calling overseas
- No need to change existing service or carrier
- No installationcharges and no monthly fee
- Fraud control
- Optional accounting codes
- Complete call detail record
- Outstanding customer service support

**Outside the United States:**
- Up to 60% savings on calls to the U.S.
- Up to 50% savings on intercontinental calls
- No installation charges
- No charge for unanswered or "busy signal" calls
- Direct dialing to almost any country
- Consecutive calls made without delay
- Complete call detail record
- Outstanding customer service and support

Telegroup Global Access
For more information, call
our Global Access department at:

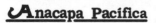

Apartado Postal 11557-1000 San José, Costa Rica, Central America
Tel:(506)255-1001 /Fax:(506) 223-6048
E-mail: anacapa@sol.racsa.co.cr

Telegroup
*Global service with a personal touch* TM

 **Association of Residents of Costa Rica**

*Formerly the Association of Pensionados and Rentistas*

## Are you, or do you wan to become, a resident in Costa Rica?
## Then join us!
### We offer you...

### For residency needs
- Service as your "bridge" to the government
- Counselling on processing of residency applications
- Renewal if ID cards and handling of periodic paperwork

### And more!
- A full range of insurance at preferred group rates
- Contacts for real estate (buy or sell) and investments
- Orientation for importing and exporting cars and household goods
- Discounts at hundreds of businesses for ARCR members
- Social and ed

### For more information

| Write | Call | Visit us in the |
|---|---|---|
| Outside Costa Rica:<br>Box025292, No.SB0019<br>Miami, FL 33102-5292<br>U.S.A<br>In Costa Rica:<br>Apdo.1068-1007 Centro Colón<br>San José | (506)233-8068<br>(506)221-2053<br>Fax:(506)222-7862<br>(506)233-1152 | "Casa Canada" Building<br>Ave.4 & 40 St. or<br>2 blocks S. of Iberia<br>Office in Paseo Colón |

# ORAL CLINIC REHABILITATION

## *Dr. Bernal Pacheco Rawson*
### *Master of Science*
Specialist in Prosthodontics
**University of Missouri - University of Costa Rica**

We give services of implant surgery and implant rehabilitation, with professional specialists in each of the fields. We also give professional specialist services in all kinds of dental treatments.

- Porcelain crown and bridges
- Complete denture
- Endodontic treatment
- Periodontal treatment
- Prosthodontic treatment
- T.M.J. and oclusion disease treatment.
- Pedodontic treatment and preventive advise
- Orthodontic treatment.

We offer a very rapid service in all crown and bridge, complete and removable partial denture because we do have our laboratory technicians in all different restorations.

**We offer security facilities and modern installations**

100 east and 50 north from A y A
Calle 11, Aves. 8 & 10
**Office: 223-7905 / Telefax:257-4735
Emergencies Bipper: 233-3333 / Home: 441-3992**

# HOSPITAL CLINICA BIBLICA

### YOUR HEALTH... OUR MAIN CONCERN

This respected Christian hospital has English-speaking doctors equipped to handle practically any emergency on a 24-hour basis.

## WE OFFER THE FOLLOWING SERVICES:

Doctors' Offices: Family Practice, Gynecology-Obstetrics, Internal Medicine, Ophthalmology, Orthopedics, Otorhinolaryngology, Pediatrics, Geriatrics, Psychiatry.

- Pharmacy 24 hours per day.
- Full-service hospitalization.
- Maternity.
- Complete laboratory analysis.
- **X-Ray, Ultrasound, Mammogram.**
- Intensive Care Coronary Unit.
- Electrocardiogram.
- Electroencephalogram.
- **Traditional Major/Minor Surgery.**
- Laparoscopic Surgery.
- Arthroscopic Surgery.
- Holter monitoring, 24 hours.
- Eco Doppler Cardiac Analysis.
- Pathology, Cytology laboratory.
- **C.A.T. Scanning.**
- Hemodyalisis.
- Hemodynamia.
- Stress Test.
- **Clinical Nutritionist.**
- Immunization, Vaccination.

**NEW SERVICES:** MRI Respiratory Function Test

Note: Our patients find that costs here are generally significantly lower than charges for comparable private medical care in North America and Europe

**Hospital phone:** (506) 257-5252 - Fax: (506) 255-4947
**Emergencies Phone:** (506) 257-0466 - Fax: (506) 223-7676
**Mailing Address:** P.O. Box 1307-1000, San José, Costa Rica
**Toll Free:** 800-911-0800
**Location:** Ave 14, Calle Central & 1

# Are you *moving?*

*You* don't have to worry about anything...

*We* will take care of every detail to make it easier for you!!

With 28 years of experience, we give you the best service!

We are specialized in the complete and integrated service of local and international moving and relocation:

customs brokers, bonded warehouse, record and furniture storage, transcar, distribution and logistics, forklift rental.

**Affiliates all around the world!**

### Telephone: (506) 224-2525

Fax: (506) 253-3390 • P.O. Box 6540-1000
email: mundanzas@sol.racsa.co.cr
San José, Costa Rica

**MUNDANZAS MUNDIALES, S.A.**

The full-service moving company in Costa Rica!

**WORLDWIDE MOVING**

# $$$ Unique Opportunity

## KANES & KANES S.A.

### GOLD COAST ESTATES

Located exactly in the middle of Costa Rica's two most famous and beautiful beaches, CONCHAL and FLAMINGO, Kanes & Kanes invites you to visit our newest project at Playa Brasilito, with 1 1/2 kilometers frontage on a new Flamingo paved road and one kilometer of beach. Even 5 years ago it would have been impossible to buy land fronting a paved road with all of the services and the amenities that are available today ... now being offered for as little as $10 per square meter, and up.

Considering the fantastic features of the area, golf course, marina, luxury hotel resort, pristine white sand beaches, where average land values run from $30 to $150 per square meter it is no wonder that we can offer only a limited number of one hectare lots at just $12 per square meter. Other offerings include smaller residential and commercial properties with convenient access to the beach as well as spectacular panoramic ocean view terraces. Commercial center locales, development parcels at very low introductory prices. Financing is also available at low interest rates. This may be your last chance... Don't miss it!! CALL NOW!!

### TEAK PLANTATION

We believe we have something never before offered in Costa Rica just seven kilometers from TAMARINDO and four kilometers from AVELLANAS BEACH near the little village of San José de Pinilla, where we have sub-divided and reforested with TEAK, 40 private title lots one hectare each. Every lot is planted with 800 trees with half the lot left open so you may build a home and recreational facility for your enjoyment. All weather roads, water and electricity are in place. A security and tree maintenance package are also part of the deal. Most people have heard about the fantastic profit projections of teak as a commodity investment and about the steady growth of land prices in the area, but the best thing about this unique opportunity is that it is selling for only $3.50 per square meter with the possibility of paying 20% down and the balance in 36 monthly payments at 10% interest on the balance. Canadian citizens enjoy a tax deductible write-off.

**For More Information or brochure visit or call us:
Kanes & Kanes Corporate Office**

Calle 17, Ave. 8 y 10, No 845, San José, Costa Rica
Tel: (506) 257-5352 or 257-5620, Fax: (506) 257-7385

# GOLDY PONCHNER GELLER

## ATTORNEY AT LAW

*University of Costa Rica*
*University of Tulane at New Orleans*
*University of Las Condes at Chile*

Offers all types of legal services and counseling in matters such as real estate, taxes, immigration, corporations, leases, litigations, contracts and business.

**English and Spanish spoken**

**Phone: 256-2601**
**Fax: 257-0694**

# BUSINESS SERVICE CENTER

Where *"SERVICE"* is our middle name!

- ❖ **Graphic Design Service:**
  Complete graphic services for all your marketing needs.
- ❖ **Costa Rica Classifieds:**
  Advertise it or sell it on the World Wide Web. We cover the world!
- ❖ **Tourist Services:**
  Luggage storage, maps, or just general assistance.
- ❖ **Fax and Mail Service:**
  Send and receive faxes, mail and courier service.
- ❖ **Catalog Service:**
  Can't find it in town? We have over 250 catalogs - From soup to nuts, including the kitchen sink!

**Is your mail important to you?**
**It is to us - we're ....**

# EXPRESS NETWORK

*Are you tired of lost mail, late mail, missing magazines and lame excuses? If you are, come into the **Business Service Center** and find out what sets us apart from the rest....*

**Tel: (506) 258-1240**
**Fax: (506) 258-0989**

North side of the Iglesia la Soledad, in the same building as the Tico Bus. Look for the Express Network sign on the door (#923).

e-mail: busercen@sol.racsa.co.cr • Internet: www.westnet.com/costarica/classifieds.html

**SAN JOSE OFFICE**
Oficentro Ejecutivo #5
San José
Mailing address:
P.O. Box 3214-1000
San José, Costa Rica

*Above the Crowd!*®

# BUYING IN COSTA RICA?

Are you overwhelmed by a lack of knowledge, customs, language or culture?
Are you concerned about security?
Whom do you trust?
Does buying here work the same as in North America?

Then let Les and Cynthia answer these questions and more. With over 15 years of North American and Costa Rican experience, we'll make it easy for you.

**Asfisa**

Phone: (506) 290-3183
Fax: (506) 296-4358
e-mail: rmasfisa@sol.racsa.co.cr
Internet: http//www.remaxcarib.com

### CALL US TODAY!

[English and Spanish]

Les Núñez   Cynthia Castro

*"Together we're better"*

- Member Chamber of Real Estate in Costa Rica
- Member Canadian Real Estate Association (CREA)
- Member National Association of Realtors (NAR) U.S.A.

# *Official Guide Books Order Form*

| | | |
|---|---|---|
| The Official Guide to Living & Making Money in Costa Rica | US $15.00 | _____ |
| The Official Guide to Living & Making Money in Mexico | US $15.00 | _____ |
| The Official Guide to Living & Making Money in Central America (Panama, Belize, El Salvador, Honduras, Guatemala, Nicaragua) | Available early 1998 | |
| The Official Guide to Living & Making Money in Cuba | Available early 1998 | |
| The Official Guide to Living & Making Money in the Caribbean | Available early 1998 | |

$2.50 for postage and handling for the first book, $1.00 for each additional book                _____

TOTAL ENCLOSED                _____

Check for Rush ☐

Make check payable to:

Lawrence International
PO Box 2062
Vashon Island, Washington 98070
206-567-4037

**Credit Card Orders Only Call:
800-341-2510, ext. 27**

Or order through our Web site: www.livingoverseas.com

## *Meet an Overseas Entrepreneur...*

Creator and director of the Official Guide Series, Robert Lawrence Johnston III was a vice president with Coldwell Banker Commercial Real Estate Company in California before moving to Costa Rica in 1992.

Taking his own advice, he started a business "offshore" in Costa Rica to take advantage of the region's low cost-of-living, perfect climate and growing business opportunities, without the taxes and overregulation of back home.

With computers, faxes, internet, overnight mail, cellular phones and daily flights to and from the U.S., more and more people are finding it easier to benefit from the opportunities in emerging markets...

...And don't forget about Uncle Sam's gift to U.S. expatriates: Totally tax-free income up to $70,000!